BOOK POWER

A Platform for Writing, Branding, Positioning, & Publishing

Kytka Hilmar-Jezek

Cover Design: April Sanson
Interior Layout: Sunny DiMartino
Design: Zanna Jezek and Sunny DiMartino
Set in Minion.

Cataloging-in-publication data for this book is available from the Library of Congress.
ISBN 13: 978-0615771779
ISBN 10: 0615771777
    1. Writing 2. Branding 3. Platform 4. Internet and Web Culture 5. Social Media
    for Business 6. Marketing 7. Product Management

Be More Network books are available at a special discount for bulk purchases in the United States by corporations, institutions, and other organizations. For more information, please contact the marketing department at:

Be More Network,
444 Brickell Avenue, Plaza 51, Suite 283,
Miami, FL 33131.
Telephone: (888) 406-5432.
Email: publishing@bemorenetwork.com.

10 9 8 7 6 5 4 3 2

PRAISE FOR BOOK POWER

"*Book Power* is just that: a book that shows you the power of your book beyond your book. Learn how to build a platform from your book. Brand and position yourself for greater reach, impact, profits, and success. Kytka does what she does best here and that is help you WIN!"

—*Louis Lautman, Executive Producer of* The YES Movie, *the film that exposes the secrets of today's youngest millionaires, TheYESmovie.com*

"Having a book is your ticket to creating a more powerful expert status, authority, and positive brand. It's something most people think is beyond them. It's not. *Book Power* provides not only the strategic thought process of the WHYs but also many of the nuts and bolts to get it done now instead of putting it off. You can turn writing your own book into a game worth winning."

—*Yanik Silver, MaverickMBA.com*

"We are currently in a perfect storm, a time where many people are craving inspiring information and many people have an inspiring message to share. The most effective way to do this is through books and the Internet. In *Book Power*, Kytka has broken this process down to an easy-to-understand and easy-to-apply complete system for anyone who has a burning desire to share their experience and insights with the world. Her information is comprehensive and applicable to this modern era of social media and online marketing . . . the leveling field for authors of all kinds. If you are ready to share your gifts with humanity, start reading this book now!"

—*Natalie Ledwell, Author of* Never in Your Wildest Dreams, *Speaker, and Co-Founder of MindMovies.com*

"If you've ever felt compelled to write a book and successfully share your message with the world, this book is for you! In *Book Power*, Kytka reveals the perfect roadmap to not only get you started but to help you complete the process. She outlines how you can create a bestseller by using positioning and a powerful platform. She teaches you how to develop a winning book AND a full product line around your knowledge! This book is invaluable for any author that is ready to succeed is today's marketplace. I highly recommend it!"

—*Cari Murphy, Host of* The Cari Murphy Show, *Soul Success Coach, Media Host, and Bestselling Author, CariMurphy.com*

"*Book Power* is a must-read. Whether you have considered writing a book or not, this will change your view of books, the power of books and completely demystifies what writing a book entails. You will be inspired to get your own expertise on paper as quickly as possible. Kytka could only do more if she wrote your book for you."

—*James Carter, Founder and CEO, Be Legendary.com*

"Everyone has a book in them, an expertise they love and are passionate about. When you write a book on your niche there is a power beyond the book, a credibility that come with that achievement. Kytka walks you through the process of bringing your ideas and expertise into action and onto paper and then building a platform around your book to share your message with the masses."

—*Craig Handley, ListenUpEspanol.com*

"Most so-called branding experts can barely explain what a personal brand is. Not only does Kytka make this easy to understand but she has gamified the process of writing a book to brand yourself and create a platform, making it straightforward and fun for anyone to create real passive income."

—*Greig Wells, LinkedIn Author and Job Search Expert, BeFoundJobs.com*

"The time is now to make your 'mess' your message; to turn your passion into profits and make work synonymous with fun and freedom—and Kytka shows you how. *Book Power* is a comprehensive, user-friendly how-to guide that will not only help you take your dreams to fruition but will show you how to collectively create, design, and market your book with your family. A family that plays together, stays together."

—*Farhana Dhalla, Author of #1 International Bestselling book*
Thank You for Leaving Me, FarhanaDhalla.com

"If ever you wanted to write a book but have been overwhelmed or unsure how to, then this is the book you need to buy. Kytka has helped me write my own book as well create many other products in a professional, easy-to-follow manner. Kytka has a gift for guiding you through the process at your own pace in a simplified system that eases you through the whole process."

—*Anil Gupta, Relationship Expert, AnilGuptaInspires.com*

"Most people don't seem to sufficiently appreciate the authority that writing your own book delivers or the exponential leverage that branding adds to your results. Those who do, often give up on the idea of writing a book, because it seems like such a monumental task! Kytka skillfully steers you through these processes, making it not only painless but actually fun to write a book and build your brand."

—*Willie Crawford, Joint Venture Broker, Mentor, and*
International Speaker, WillieCrawford.com

"After two decades of serving people to embrace self and service leadership, my greatest blessing has been to share the messages of those souls who have taken their life's greatest adversities and turned them into their gifts. Kytka is one of those great souls who has not just turned her life around for herself and her family, she has taken her gift to serve others in a massive way. *Book Power* is a results-based system that covers everything we need to become published authors in today's world and position our work and ourselves in a way that adds massive value to even more people!"

—*Harry Singha, Author of* WTF Is Going On? How To Turn Our Worst Days Into Our Best Days, *Chairman of the Youth Coaching Academy Global, HarrySingha.com*

"I have been in the personal development, branding, and marketing industry for 25 years. Kytka and her amazing family are beyond wise and talented when it comes to writing, branding, marketing, and expert creativity. They have added tremendous value to several of my projects, and I would consider their talent far above most in the development of personal wealth and success industry."

—*Gary King, Author and Speaker, ThePowerofTruth.com, TheHappinessFormula.tv*

"I have known Kytka for years, and here are a few things about her that I know are true. Few people take action and pursue goals in life and business to the fullest. Kytka is one of those who has struggled in life and been knocked down but got up and moved forward and persevered. More importantly she works daily to help motivate and inspire others to do the same. This book is a blueprint of how anyone can utilize the modern technology and concepts and get their ideas, causes, products, and services out to the world and make a difference. In *Book Power*, Kytka doesn't only give you the why but the how through actionable items that are broken into steps anyone can follow and implement. If getting your message and ideas is what you wanted to do, especially in the form of a book, then *Book Power* is for you."

—*Dan Stojadinovic. Dan helps people craft their message into inspirational presentations that tell stories and move people. HowToMakePresentations.com*

"There are two significant characteristic in social media and marketing: clarity and engagement. Kytka understands that clarity is equally critical in product creation. Kytka delivers an engaging and simple method for the creation of a book that anyone can follow."

—*Ginger Rockey-Johnson, The Spice Girl of Tampa Bay, Radio Show Host, Concierge Marketing Agency Expert, SpiceGirlofTampaBay.com*

For everyone who has ever had the dream to
do more, live more, and be more.

And for those who go beyond that dream.

TABLE OF CONTENTS

ACKNOWLEDGMENTS

I have the deepest gratitude to those around me who have been instrumental in the completion of this book. Without your inspiration, encouragement, and guidance, this project would not have materialized. I'm especially grateful to:

My mother and father, for launching me into this world and instilling in me a love of living on my terms.

My children, Zynnia, Zanna, and Zachary, for keeping my focus on the future, for the adventures and laughter, and for the sunshine you bring into each and every day.

My partners, Robert and Jane, for the support, opportunities, and Southern hospitality.

Tony, for having my back.

My family: Pavel, for holding down the fort. Kati and Joel, for our home away from home. Scott, for Zachary's West Coast abode. Vlasta for surviving. Tom, David, Sabrina, and Richulka, for always opening the door. Helen, for the yellow butterflies. Babi Marie, for watching over us and telling us the show must go on.

My mentors and friends: Brendon Burchard, for the charge. Simon Sinek, for the why. Gary Vaynerchuk, for the crush. Vishen Lahkiani, for his vision. Yanik Silver, for his entrepreneurial excellence. Bri and Arielle Ford, for their love. Taylor Conroy, for being a change hero. Greig Wells, for being linked in. Anil Gupta, for mastery. Willie Crawford, for his joint venture brokering excellence and soul food. Anthony Robbins, for kicking my ass. Astrid Witt, for education. Brian Scrone and Jim Sheils, for the board meetings. Denise Cassino, for her #1 skills. Louis Lautman, for the youngest entrepreneurs. Gary King, for character. Laura Brown, for reaching out. Moriah Diamond, for capturing awesomeness. Jason Henderson, for big bunnies. Greg Jacobs, for being a Jedi Master. Cory Boatright, for being real. Shawn Royster, for keeping the show on the road. Amish Shah, for his honest posts. Lisa Nichols, for that smile. Mitch Sanders, for strategic deviance. Michael Drew, for pendulum. Drew Canole, for back flips. Chad Mureta, for apps. Leanne Beesley, for her cheery smile. Len Branson, for being super wise. Harry Singha, for his commitment to youth worldwide. Jeff Marx, for all of the hugs.

James Carter, for being legendary. Jonathan Budd, for saying no to vacuuming. Lynne Twist, for Pachamama. Burt Goldman, for quantum jumping. Elliot Kay, for keeping the hat on. William Lee, for always making time. Natalia Almeida, for creating a happy space. Landon Ray, for always saying hello. Emily Tu, for her deepest sharing. Jessica Langdon, for seeing truth. Jamie Mintun, for shining as a survivor. Greg Campisi, for reminding us love is all around. Adam Piplica, for magical pennies. Amanda Wright-Hughes, for getting what you want. Ballardo Zuniga, for putting the "pura" back into "vida." Jairek Robbins, for that smile and keeping an eye on Zynnia. Malek Houlihan, for making the guitar sing. Kainoa Horcajo, for aloha spirit. Joe Polish, for his piranha marketing. Aaron Darko, for futuristic innovation. Sheryl Nicholson, for being Superwoman. Linda Burhans, for her gentle guidance. Andrew Hewitt, for game changers. Kyle Cease, for being funny and true.

Farhana Dhalla, for her listening ear. Craig Handley, for bringing his awesome kids. Chris Attwood, for time at the luau. Natalie and Glenn Ledwell, for mind movies. Kaileen Apple, for bringing Zynnia on stage. Veena Sidhu, for her beauty inside and out. Johnny Wall, for conversations at the villa. Leanne and Alexandra, for their juicy genius. Sammy Taggett, for his music. Vivian Glyck, for her amazing work with children. John Colandrea, for his fantastic pizza and smile. Gabriel Oliva, for time with Zack. Lara Berg, for her Brightside yoga. Ginger Rockey-Johnson, for being the spiciest girl. Joel Bauer, for pink persuasion. Dan Stojadinovic, for his genuine immigration story. Christine Chang, for living her dream through the lens. Tiffany and November Persons, for Sierra Leone. Cari Murphy, for creating change now. Chris Krimitson, for the spotlights. Topher Morrison, for NLP and insights shared. Scott Tischler, for being my diamond guy. And to the rest who are unnamed: You know who you are and how much you mean to me.

My students: You allow me to see my strengths through your continuing successes. Rebecca, for the honorable title of sensei.

My community and tribe, for offering me their trust and relationships.

You, the reader, for playing a bigger game.

The guidance and support I have received from all the amazing people I am blessed to have had cross my path. I am grateful to each and every one of you for your constant support and help.

My deepest gratitude . . .

INTRODUCTION

An invitation to play a new game lies within these pages. By playing, your life will change, and once you understand how to play this game you will want to share it with others. This is the definitive game changer for your personal and professional life.

Before we begin, let me ask you a few questions. Where do you stand now in your sector or business? Are you discouraged with how hard the economy has hit? Are you scratching your head wondering how to get yourself more attention, more leads, more clients? Maybe you've seen some in your sector win, while others die the quiet death of closing down, disappearing into oblivion, into the land of game over. Have you noticed that the game you played before has changed? With social media on the rise and new technologies coming out each and every day, do you wonder how you will ever win?

No matter where you are now, there is hope. Within these pages lie a powerful game plan and manual to the elusive world of authors, speakers, and experts. *Book Power* is the playbook that defines each step of the path to positioning yourself as the authority in your field. At the end of the game, you will have authored a book, know how to brand and market yourself, and be ready to launch a winning platform. You will master the combination of all of these tools to powerfully position yourself as the winning expert in your field. You will win.

Today's winners are the players who rise to the top, the ones who are the most seen and heard. But do you ever stop to consider *why* we choose to turn our focus to them in the first place? What makes them winning experts? I repeat: It is a special combination of branding, positioning, and publishing on a congruent platform aligned with their unique message. They didn't get there by luck; they knew how to play their position.

This book has been written to give you the necessary plays to succeed. I share a fun and easy-to-use formula to write a quality book quickly while educating you on how to strategically combine today's social media channels with your website to give you the greatest visibility and reach. In this book, I teach you how to win.

With your expertise, knowledge, passion, intention, and attention, you will finish and publish your book in weeks, instead of the years it normally would take by following the traditional agent and publisher route. This, combined with the other plays, will give you the winner's advantage. Everyone has a unique gift, a unique combination of traits. NOW is the time to publish your book! Now is the time to brand yourself, empower yourself, and to share your gift with the world!

> Each of us is a unique strand in the intricate web of life and is here to make a contribution.
>
> ▶ *Deepak Chopra*

In this book I offer you creative directions on writing your book, creating your product, branding yourself, and strategically developing your platform as a whole. You will attain authority, credibility, and respect for being an expert. Doors that you never even knew existed will open.

As a result of utilizing your book as a positioning tool and aligning it with your brand and platform, your business will flourish. You will quickly rise in your field and be in a position to tap into a lifetime flow of residual income. I know this exists for you, and I guarantee that you will love the grand new adventure you are embarking upon.

So turn the page and begin now!

FOREWORD

In today's publishing world, all bets are off.

You can self-publish easily. But once the book is up there, what happens to it? Many authors simply cross their fingers, hope for the best and wait for the returns to come in. Most of them are still waiting.

Writing and publishing a book might be easier than ever, thanks to Amazon, Barnes & Noble and a host of self-publishing sites. But that doesn't mean it's any easier either to write or to promote a book. And many people who want to write a book have little idea about how to begin.

That's where Kytka Hilmar-Jezek comes in. She has proposed in "*Book Power*" a way to get your thoughts organized into a book, and a method to getting your book noticed. And why your book is so important to your future business.

She charts a course for your publishing path, through various self-publishing options through which you can bring your ideas to market. She also suggests something a little unusual: that creating your book, and publishing your book, can be an enjoyable experience almost as if you were playing a game.

This is not what most people expect to hear when they read about book publishing, which is a cutthroat business where you're either a bestseller or consigned to the dust heap of forgotten or never-seen titles. But by making the creation, publishing and promoting of your book a game-like experience, you'll likely devote more time to doing what you need to do to get your book—and you—noticed by the reading public. And the consumer who wants to know you better. You want to be more than noticed—you want to make a difference and to sell books.

Hilmar-Jezek discusses branding, positioning and building a platform for yourself—all without making it seem like heavy lifting. You'll build your team, identify your allies, embark on your course, utilize your platform, build your credibility and more.

It sounds a little vague, but Hilmar-Jezek gives you the particulars you will need to move ahead. So put on your game face and dive in. She gives you the power to become more successful through a valuable extension of who you are: your book.

—*Bob Hughes*

Robert J. Hughes was a staff reporter for The Wall Street Journal for over a decade, specializing in culture reporting. He was the paper's theater reporter, wrote on publishing, the art and auction markets, television, music, film and philanthropy, and reviewed books.

THE GAME

We are a very playful species, and study after study shows that we learn best when at play. When we have a feeling of doing what we love, the day seems to fly by, and tasks feel effortless to complete. "That was easy!" we think to ourselves.

What if all of life were simply a game, with nothing to get all worked up about? What if everything were as easy as play?

I'm about to show you a way that it can be and to provide you with the tools to make it easier than you ever imagined. If you play along, you will have written a book by the end of this game. You will have the information you need to go forth at a whole new level. Do you want to come and play? What if I also give you an all-access pass and tell you that at the end of the game you can win a better life for yourself and your family? Would you want to come and play then?

When we play, we are in our natural state. Much of what we do when in that play space comes from something called "being in flow."

> Flow is the mental state of operation in which a person performing an activity is fully immersed in a feeling of energized focus, full involvement, and enjoyment in the process of the activity. In essence, flow is characterized by complete absorption in what one does.
>
> ▶ *Mihaly Csikszentmihalyi*

To make the experience of being in today's game more engaging and to motivate you to move through quickly and effectively, this book has been formatted using a methodology called gamification.

Gamification is the use of game-thinking and game mechanics in non-game contexts in order to engage users and solve problems. Gamification is used in applications and processes to improve user engagement, ROI, data quality, timeliness, and learning.

▶ *Wikipedia*

By the end of 2010, website product managers and marketers alike were using gamification as a tool to test the engagement of their customers. They found that gamification encouraged desirable usage. One group, DevHub, added gamification elements to their online tasking and noticed a consistent 70% increase in performance and completion.

The employees who were given the opportunity to do their jobs in game form not only played but played to win. They had fun completing their tasks, reported being happier at work, and got their daily workloads completed on time and often before deadline. That's it; a simple tweak in perception, and workers become engaged players who produce 70% more than before. Amazing, isn't it?

How would your life change if you had a 70% increase in the completion of your projects and the quality of your performance? How different would your world be? Do you ever think about it? I'm sure you do. And then you quickly talk yourself out of it, convincing yourself that it's too hard. But what if it is only a game—a game you can learn to play and to win?

What if the game were explained in a way where you become a champion of the playing field and rack up perks and bonuses almost immediately? What if all of the confusion were taken out of the game, and each operation and mission were explained so simply that you would find yourself wondering why you waited so long to play?

> This is the real secret of life–to be completely engaged with what you are doing in the here and now. And instead of calling it work, realize it is play.
>
> ▸ *Alan Wilson Watts*

What if you love playing this game so much that you want to teach it to your family, friends, and loved ones? How much better could their lives become?

I challenge you to play this game and to move one level at a time with the overall goal of completing each level, mission, and operation until you win. Are you ready to play?

Game on!

PLAY TO WIN

You've heard this before: "It doesn't matter if you win or lose, it's how you play the game."

We play the game for the sake of playing, but we also play to win. Immersion in playing games is not a new concept; it's just evolved in the digital era. Humans have played games since the beginning of time. It's what we do.

According to the Greek historian Herodotus, the kingdom of Lydia employed nation-wide gaming as a solution to starvation and chaos in the streets during a famine. They rotated their schedule by eating one day and playing games on the next. Due to the immersive nature of games, they managed to survive this way for 18 years, when they otherwise would have likely perished.

The Lydians played, and they won, in this case, their lives. So while we play for the fun of it, we also play to win. The secret is that we have incorrectly defined winning.

The *American Heritage Dictionary* defines winning this way:

> Verb: To acquire as a result of one's actions, behavior, or effort. Getting, gaining, earning, deserving, meriting. (i.e., to move towards)

Verb: To come into possession of. Getting, obtaining, coming by, gaining, acquiring, landing, securing, picking up, procuring. (i.e., to get)

Verb: To obtain possession or control of. Taking, getting, gaining, capturing. (i.e., to control)

To become a winner, one has to take the action of moving towards gaining, capturing, and controlling.

It's really very straightforward. Go after what you want until you get it, and if you succeed at that which you attempt, then, by definition, you are a winner. In other words, you will become a winner simply by playing all the way through.

Your prize? You will have an average of a 70% increase, based on DevHub's study, in who you will be when you come out on the other end of this game. But you have to play, and you can't quit!

If we apply this to today's business landscape, we become aware that most people are simply refusing to play. They are intimidated by the new technology and feel overwhelmed at the thought of learning it all. Because they refuse to play, they are no longer seen, because the eyes and ears of today are focused on a completely different playing field. Players get frustrated and exhausted wondering what they are doing wrong without realizing that they are sitting on the bench by their own choice. Business today is played on a whole new game board.

Those on the bench still have the old playbooks, and each year more and more are discovering the old plays no longer apply. They find out the hard way and often too late, many declaring bankruptcy and losing their homes along with their hope. In the old days, the rules were simple and the game was even simpler. By just showing up on the field and with a little sweat, you could play. But today, what field is the game on? Where do we play first? How does this game tie into the old game and its old rules? Players get overwhelmed and retreat to the sidelines, passively watching while others win and win big.

Technology has brought the game to our laptops and mobile phones. We see everyone playing on the fields of Twitter, Facebook, Pinterest, YouTube, and LinkedIn. We want to play too, but no matter how we try to join the game, it seems to be moving in fast forward, and we just cannot seem to catch up. We get frustrated and think it is "game over" for us. We forget that to play is to win.

How you play your game can be modeled after sports, war games, card games, spy games, or cooperative board games; whichever you are happiest to play. My personal favorites are spy and detective games, so while I do mix some metaphors in the book, I focus on special operations, missions, and levels for you to complete this game of writing your book and building your platform.

The point is to drop the unnecessary weight and the things that are holding you back. Play your book into being; make it a game. It's not complicated; you simply need to know how to make you presence in the game known.

Step in as a valuable asset to the game, and play your biggest and best game each and every time. Be real and unique, because you bring something to the game that was not there before.

We look at the players who are winning and try to copy them. We try to get a website and some social media channels, but it still isn't working. Why? Because we each have our own position, and we cannot play as someone else.

> Don't compare yourself with anyone in this world . . . If you do so, you are insulting yourself.
>
> ▸ *Bill Gates*

To set yourself apart, you need to play a brand-new position, the one life's game has reserved exclusively for you. You may not believe you qualify, but I know you do. Who you play as is determined by your uniqueness. The maker created only one of you, and your life's journey and experience have placed you in a very interesting position. To play, you must take what you already have and know and build a personal player who defines a unique brand. This book is about the winning advantages of offering your unique proposition to the world. It is about magnifying your greatness by giving you more visibility.

The plays in this book will create a funnel for lead generation for your business and teach you how to target your followers in a specific way to ensure success. It will show you how to finally separate yourself from following the herd by positioning yourself as the leader and authority in your field. Although my students accomplish the missions laid out in this book within 10 days, you may decide to spread it out over 30 days. The important thing is that you play all the way to the end.

The methods presented here are not some sort of "get rich quick scheme," nor will they make you millions overnight. What you will learn to do is to play bigger and better. You will write a real book that will introduce you to the world in a grand, impactful way. This book will be your new business card. It will position you at an advantage where you gain credibility and an additional residual income stream that adds up over time, with no extra work on your part. This can help you strengthen relationship with your clients and open the door to new conversations and opportunities.

The extra funds that come regularly can be used to save for your child's education, pay off debt, get that "cash deal" on your new vehicle, buy all of the cool toys you want, and even quit your day job. Once you learn to play this game, you will never have to work another day in your life, because everything you do from this day forth will be continuing to play the game.

In the near future, your play will be used as a springboard for expanding your presence to include a full line of products and services built around you as the brand. These include products, services, coaching, workshops, speaking engagements, interviews, and much more. Playing as an author/expert will open doors that have previously been closed, and you will be well on your way to living the winning life of your dreams.

If you are tired of doing business as usual and ready to play a much bigger game, you are ready for this book and its invitation to play.

Winners don't wait for chances—they take them.

START NOW

> You are an expert in something, but does the rest of the world know? You have a wealth of information, experience, and knowledge that you can package into a book that will benefit others. This truly is the information age, and people want to know what you know.
>
> ▶ *Denise Hamilton*

Have you ever considered yourself an expert? If you answered yes, then good for you—I hope you have a book telling others how you do what you do. If you answered no, then I challenge you to spend the next couple of hours reading this book and then, in the next 10 days, implementing what you've learned here. When you realize the value of the impact your book will make, your decision to write will be a no-brainer!

Either way, now is the best possible time to get started writing your book. More than that, by using this very simple, powerful system, you will soon be thinking about your second book and your third book and beyond. You will want to recruit your spouse, children, and parents to write their own books. You will understand that everyone has a unique voice whose legacy can be forever captured in print.

The key is to begin. Dreaming about getting started is not going to make it happen. Action is everything. So make a promise to yourself to commit and take action.

IDENTITY

This book is both a resource and a training guide. It will give you the information, guidance, tools, and motivation to write your own book. Your book is a springboard and an integral strategic part of your overall game plan. Being an author positions you strongly upon your platform. It is the passport for starting you on your journey to becoming the recognized authority in the field or space where you work or aspire to work. I know I keep repeating this, but you must understand how writing a book will change your life.

Whether you are a doctor, lawyer, professional, product developer, speaker, coach, housewife, unemployed, or have a "how-to system" in place, this timely information will help get you seen and heard by the people who value your expertise and experience. By the end of this book you will understand the importance of branding, positioning, authoring, and building a platform across many channels. You will be able to see a clear roadmap to where you want to go and how to get there.

There is a special prestige that authors enjoy, and just by writing a book they stand out in their marketplace (I'll be calling it "space"). Authors have a strong influence on their target markets and gain credibility as an expert in their topic or field. This is a natural by-product of authoring a book, and that is why writing your book is so very important and should be at the top of your "to do" list.

By authoring a book, your income will increase, incrementally at first, and then all of sudden more rapidly, when you learn the sequencing of what should align with your book authorship.

Let me illustrate this by sharing a story. A few years ago, after co-organizing a brilliant presentation by Gary Vaynerchuk, the author of the bestselling book *Crush It*, I wanted to invite another thought leader to speak to our group, the Wealth Building Annex. Somewhere I had heard about Gary's "Circle of Influence," and I was captivated by his presentation of how leaders inspire action. I contacted Simon Sinek, a well-known speaker and author who wrote the book *Start With Why*. It was late 2009, and I tentatively booked him to speak at a conference for approximately $1,500.

When I contacted Simon again a few weeks later to make final arrangements, I reached a personal representative who informed me that after his recent TED Talk appearance, his popularity and demand had gone through the roof; hence, the new speaking fee was $25,000! That was in October 2009. Out of curiosity, I just did a quick online search to find that his current fees are between $40,00 and $60,000 (source: SpeakerMix).

"Visibility Is The Name of The Game"

Your book will also be a huge impetus in positioning you as the expert in your community and for your market space. As your credibility grows, so will your circle of influence. The tools I give you here will help you brand and position your expert and authoritative status in your field and in the areas where you want to work.

WHY

Having read this far, I'm sure you're getting excited about playing the game. You now know the significance of putting the value of what you know into the world. Playing the game will instruct you on how to express your voice when you write about your personal brand and positioning. Now you must focus on what you will write about and narrow your subject matter. I call this process "chunking it down" (i.e., breaking it down into small, bite-sized chunks). I am confident you have many things you could teach and write about, but for this specific game play, what is it you wish to convey and why?

> Always start with why"
>
> ▶ *Simon Sinek*

Why is it important that you write this book? When you have clarity and focus, you are ready to begin to play. You must be crystal clear as to why you are writing this book. My hope is that you are writing this book because you know you have something unique and valuable to share with the world—not only to position yourself as the trusted authority in your space. If you want a free play to grow your business, the book will help, but it will not last if you are not writing with the intention to share what you know. Don't hoard your information; put out your very best and see how others appreciate and recommend you.

When you know your why, then focus on what you intend your book to do for you. I don't mean this in a selfish way, where you don't care about the content and are focused only on personal gains. Instead, I want you to begin to envision yourself as an expert, a trusted authority, and an author who is being asked to share expertise. When you see yourself as already being there, your writing will flow from the very best part inside you.

This is your nonfiction book in the area of your experience and knowledge, a book of your life's experience and know-how. You are creating a game plan for others on a similar journey, and you will offer them an easier path by sharing what you know. Your intention is for readers to benefit from your experiences and avoid the costly and time-consuming mistakes you may have made. You want to help your readers learn the shortcuts and what you would have avoided and why.

As you write, keep a clear sense of why writing this is important to you but also share your why within the body of the book. Why do your readers need to take the steps you describe? Are you saving them time, money, resources? Why did you start your journey to begin with? Did you want to change the world or get from point A to point B? Why did you keep going, even when it was difficult? Was there a light at the end of the tunnel, a reward at the end? Why should they hang in there?

All of these things will work magic if implemented correctly and consistently.

LIKE CLOCKWORK

Every wealthy person I've ever met has several revenue streams going at one time. Each and every month, like clockwork, their passive income arrives. This just makes sense, because you never know when something can happen that changes your circumstances. If your entire livelihood depends on that one paycheck you bring in from your job, what happens if you lose your job, if the company closes, or if your job gets outsourced?

Doesn't it make sense to have several income streams flowing in your direction each and every month, a dependable passive income, residual, or royalty income from somewhere? You bet it does!

In the next couple of chapters I will discuss branding, positioning, and building a platform. I am strategically placing these at the front of the book because you can use the information to write your book in your brand voice and in a way that will align with your brand message and platform. So even though you are ready to get started writing, please do not skip through the next chapters, as they are an important part of why you are writing and how you will present yourself in your book and beyond.

NEW BUSINESS CARD

What do you hold in your hand that weighs approximately one pound, measures 6 × 9 inches, and has your name written all over it? The answer is your book, which is also your new business card.

An increasing number of people are taking advantage of having a leg up on their competition by branding themselves as "the expert" in their particular niche. Call it a business card, a resume, a billboard, or whatever you choose, but the long and short of it is that books are no longer just books. They are branding devices and credibility builders, not to mention door openers. Books are the reason that authors command large speaking and consulting fees.

> Thanks in large part to the explosion of Indie book publishing, the use of the book as a business card has added a new and powerful tool to the marketing arsenal of many successful business people. For a few hundred dollars, seasoned experts and professionals are putting their knowledge into professionally-published books–a calling card sure to make a much bigger impression than the traditional business card.
>
> ▶ *Author Solutions*

As *Esquire* put it, "Books and articles for writers of the 21st century have become billboards for their messages."

Authors using book-driven branding get to the next level in their professional career much more quickly. Additionally, there is so much more to leverage from your published book. Your book and new expert status will lead to speaking engagements, consulting, trainings, and other events. At these events you will have numerous opportunities to increase your brand awareness, drive traffic to your platform, and generate sales. Every time you present yourself to an audience you have the opportunity to share yourself and your product, service, or company with the attendees long after you leave the stage, through your book and later a full line of helpful "backend products."

TEAM

LEADER

A leader is one who knows the way, goes the way, and shows the way.

▶ *John Maxwell*

It occurred to me that you may be wondering if I am qualified to write this book. My primary qualification is a genuine passion for the subject matter. I have been blessed with the ability to help numerous people write their books, position and brand themselves, and deliver it all to their client base on a solid and functional platform. I have held workshops and trainings all over the United States, often to sold-out crowds, on the subjects of building a platform for success and writing a book in 10 days. I know the way.

I have built over 120 websites and sold many of them as a "branded platform in a specific niche." I have personally authored numerous books, two of which have gone on to bestseller status: One went to #2 in two categories and another went to #5. I also taught my children to author books, and I launched my daughter's book and my son's book, both of which reached the top 50 in their categories. I know the way.

My personal time is spent furthering my own education and expertise by attending entrepreneurial, personal development, and marketing events all over the world. And I do all of the above as a single mother with three homeschooled children. Teaching them the exact skills I offer you in this book has secured my children a future where they will be in charge of their own destinies. I homeschooled my children because I want them to have a real life education. I am an entrepreneur, and I inspire them to be entrepreneurs as well. I show the way.

> The word "educate" dates back from 1447, from the Latin word: educatus, ("bring up, rear, educate,"), and which is related to educere "bring out," from ex- "out" + ducere "to lead."
>
> ▶ *Wikipedia*

In my opinion, bringing out leaders is what education is supposed to be about. Sadly, much of what we see happening today is the direct opposite. As the daughter of immigrant parents, I was brought up in a school of thought where children are integral parts of the family unit. I have raised my own children in the same way. They are my best friends and also an important and integral part of my team.

The work that I do affects them, so it is their work too, and they take a deep interest in it. Knowing the depth of how it all works causes them to have great respect for what I do and for what we do together. They value the combined efforts, and this gives them confidence and self-esteem. They are not afraid to try new things, knowing that making mistakes along the way is all a part of the learning process. As I watch them grow, I see their own strengths and individual skills develop. They are artistic, entrepreneurial-minded, and visionaries, the kind of people who create and innovate.

As a result, my own platform is expanding to the realm of education and entrepreneurialism for children, and I am now invited to speak on those subjects as well. I share this with you to illustrate how using what you know as a starting point is your best asset. As your following grows and you reach more people, you will begin to feel more confident in your own expert capabilities and the scope of what you teach will expand. Other books and programs will be created, and your income will expand with the extent of your influence.

This is also the reason you see my children in my branding—we are a team that works together. You may find it interesting to know that they are also branching into their own careers in related fields. My son is an author/speaker; my daughter is behind the scenes in video production, graphics, WordPress, and branding; and my youngest is a rising star in her own right. Did I mention that at age nine she brought the room to a standing ovation at the Super Women's Summit after her presentation on video marketing? You can view a clip of that, as well as interviews with some well-known experts on our website:

www.BeMoreThanYouAre.com

My children accompany me to all of the above mentioned events, and they have received a powerful education, which has sharpened their imaginations, built self-confidence, and shown them that anything is possible!

Perhaps my strongest qualification to lead you through this game is my drive to ensure that you realize that all you seek is actually within your own hands. I believe you just need help to understand how the new game is played. Traditional channels and belief systems hold people captive to outmoded patterns and techniques of the old games. With the technologies available today, and in a world that gets louder each day, your saving grace is to play along and write your book. Stand up as who you are and be heard. Speak with your unique voice.

The world is waiting for you!

ACCESS

Today, authors are in the idea-making business, not the book business. In short, this means that publishing a book is less about sales and much more about creating a brand. The real customers of books are no longer just readers but now include speaking agents, CEOs, investors, and startups.

▶ *Ryan Holiday, Fast Company*

Book authors are in high demand for speaking engagements and appearances; they are the new celebrity, and celebrities gain access. Authors make money not only from royalties or book advances but from their keynotes, presentations, and strategically branded product lines.

This book includes entrepreneurial ideas for you to extend yourself beyond simply writing and prepares you to add speaking and consulting to your revenue stream. You have to begin to look outside book sales and towards the speaking market. There are radio interviews, news, television, small channel television keynotes, lectures, seminars, and workshops available to you. These types of events have the possibility to be much more lucrative than just selling books. In essence, the book builds and brands you in the public eye. It gives you credibility and the opportunity to be more than you are. It enables you to now be a voice, a teacher, a leader, an expert—after all, you wrote the book on it!

ALLIES

So who will be your primary publishing ally? I recommend CreateSpace, owned by Amazon, for the simple fact that Amazon dominates the space. Working with CreateSpace is comfortable and simple. Their support of your project is without equal. With their fast approval process and print-on-demand (POD) technologies, you can get your book in your hands, realistically, for under $10 in a matter of days. Of course, you have several choices in choosing where to self-publish. The following statistics are provided by Bowker, the company that manages book identifier codes (ISBN numbers). Their statistics for 2011 show the following for self-published books:

Publisher	Number of Titles
CreateSpace	58,412
Smashwords	40,608
Author Solutions	47,094
Lulu	38,005

The obvious advantage with CreateSpace is their connection with Amazon and Kindle, in addition to being the leader in book sales (align with experts!). There are others, of course, and many traditional publishing houses are stepping into the self-publishing game, but costs are high and your book takes longer to launch.

An example of this is Balboa Press. Balboa Press is an up-and-coming contender with the power of Hay House behind them. They specialize in books with a positive message in the self-help genre, and because they are affiliated with Hay House, their authors have an automatic implied credibility worked in. Their support is excellent, and they have staff available to assist with marketing and design in addition to publishing. They are looking for paradigm shifters who are committed to human potential and enlightenment. Learn more about them and what they offer here:

www.balboapress.com/Perks/BalboaAdvantages.aspx

Considerations

When you publish with Balboa Press, you gain many positive advantages, including:

- Having your book become the next Hay House title
- Earth-friendly publishing
- Marketing options from Hay House
- Editorial standards that ensure a consistent positive message
- Association with Hay House
- Substantial author discounts
- Retaining the rights to your book
- Maintaining control at every step
- Access to expert editing and marketing services

They offer six different publishing packages priced between $999 and $7,999. The obvious advantage to a user interested in Balboa is the affiliation with Hay House, the leader in the self-help arena.

Kindle

Amazon's CreateSpace is making it very easy for authors to also publish their work in the Kindle store, and the rewards are terrific, both in terms of the financial rewards and the exposure you get with your Kindle e-book. Amazon recently raised its royalties (money that is paid to the author) for certain types of e-books to make it even more attractive to self-publish on the Kindle. You can earn up to 70% of the sale of your e-books if they qualify.

What is so great about publishing to Kindle?

- More affordable: The e-book market is growing.
- Adding new content: Easier for authors to self-publish.
- Large royalties: Incentive for authors to publish.

What are the benefits of publishing to Kindle?

Visibility

- Reach highly targeted potential customers.
- Amazon can recommend your book.
- Multiple titles = greater visibility.

Credibility

- Authors are experts, right?

Easy and Fast

- Learn and follow my system, and your next books will be easier to write. (Yes, next books!)
- English-language books can appear on Amazon in 24 hours.
- Books in foreign languages appear within two weeks (and outsourcing the translation of your book is easy and inexpensive!).

Earn Money on Autopilot

- Earn royalties for as long as your book is in the Kindle store.
- Write more books and increase your royalties.
- In newer books, remember to mention older books or announce additions to a series.

With all of the new Kindle devices, apps for iPad, iTouch, iPhone, Android, tablets, and computers, all of which can access Kindle books, you now have the ability to sell your books to almost everyone on the planet.

Amazon claimed that two years after introducing the Kindle, customers are now buying more e-books than all hard covers and paperbacks combined. In 2011, revenues from e-book sales came to more than $989 million. That figure is estimated to triple by the end of 2012 to over $3 BILLION!

> Our goal is to have every book, ever published, in any language available for Kindle customers to purchase and begin reading in less than 60 seconds. If your book is not yet available on Kindle, we'd like to help you reach this quickly growing market. If you hold the electronic rights to your book and would like to convert and sell it in the Kindle format using Amazon's self-publishing tools, visit Kindle Direct Publishing. If your publisher holds the electronic rights to your book, contact them directly and ask them to make it available to Amazon for sale on Kindle.
>
> ► *Amazon, about Kindle*

Read more on this here:

www.amazon.com/kindlepublishing

I know Amazon will succeed with this goal, and this is why you must make your book available both in print and for Kindle.

PLAYER

INITIATION

Self-publishing has become a position of power, not a position of last resort.

► *Hugh Howey, Author of Wool*

I read in an interview that Hugh Howey began writing his book while working at a bookstore. He received a modest advance from a small publisher and thought he was on his way, but days of waiting turned into weeks, then months, and the publisher simply failed to deliver. So he decided to try on his own. He began to blog about writing and his experience with it, and he began to build a small but committed following of fans. Then he wrote *Wool*, a science fiction novelette of 58 pages, which seemed to take on a life of its own. His loyal following responded, and word of mouth spread like wildfire.

Sales of his book began to go through the roof, and Hugh quickly added four more titles to his series. These days, Hugh finds himself selling 50,000+ copies per month and is making a six-figure income. Director Ridley Scott has optioned it for a movie, and Random House has announced that they are publishing the hardcover edition in the United Kingdom.

Hugh chose to play the new game, and he introduced it to his followers and his community. He wrote about it on his blog. He used his platform to launch his book. He could have gotten stuck trying to understand why the publisher failed him. He could have given up, believing his writing was insignificant to anyone. But he didn't. He played the game. He played, and he won.

> If you don't play, you don't have a chance to win. Don't think. Thinking is the enemy of creativity. It's self-conscious, and anything self-conscious is lousy. You can't try to do things. You simply must do things.
>
> ▶ *Ray Bradbury*

Hugh's success proves a theory he had about the self-publishing phenomenon even before the success of *Wool*. He says:

> With self-publishing you don't waste your time trying to get published, which can take years of query letters and agent expenses and all that entails, instead you go directly to the real gatekeepers, which are the readers. If they respond favorably and you have sales, you can leverage that into a writing career. If they don't, you start writing the next big thing. Either way you're not spending your time trying to get published, you're spending your time writing your next book.

This is a powerful strategy worth noting and imitating, an inspirational side note of what is possible. Want to know the largest advance ever paid for a self-published book? It was $4.125 million. Simon & Schuster paid that for Richard Paul Evans's *The Christmas Box*. I am sure that was a holiday gift he didn't expect! Richard didn't dream about writing a book. He took action and played the game.

Do or do not. There is no try.

▶ *Yoda*

KNOWING

Life. Experience. Having rolled up your sleeves and done it. That is what makes you an expert. We have been sold the idea that experts are people with a certain education or certain degrees, and we have downplayed the everyday people who are in the trenches each and every day, living it and doing it. Do you believe that 4 years of study offers more information than 20 years of doing? How about four years of 2 hours a week versus 40 hours a week for six months?

Who defines the true value of information? Who can separate what is important to each individual on the planet? You may have walked a life path that someone is also walking in a similar way, only you are 20 steps ahead. What is the value of knowing what to expect in those next 20 steps? How would your own life have been different had you known then what you know now?

We live in the information age. The sheer volume of it and its being available everywhere create a need for information that has value. Yes, we can look anything up on Google, but who has the time? Can we be sure that the information comes from a trustworthy source?

Your experience has given you a deep knowledge of your subject matter. You have insights and ideas that others don't. You are holding a roadmap that has great value for someone. What's stopping you from sharing your knowledge?

PUSHING THROUGH

Perhaps you have been afraid to put yourself out there because of a fear of rejection. Let me get straight to the point: Get over it right now! Ponder the following quote for a moment, and then move on with the decision to write rather than not to write, because *not* to write is not "to be." You deny yourself and your audience. You have had an incredible journey to get to where you are and have amassed experience and knowledge. Now combine that with your unique voice and be heard. You are already an expert. Accept it.

> Rejection doesn't mean you aren't good enough;
> it means the other person failed to notice the
> value and the power of what you have to offer.

It is a fact that most famous authors and their books were rejected, not just once but a multitude of times. Jack Canfield, author of the now famous *Chicken Soup* series said, "We were rejected by 123 publishers all told. The first time we went to New York, we visited with about a dozen publishers in a two-day period with our agent, and nobody wanted it. They all said it was a stupid title, that nobody bought collections of short stories, that there was no edge—no sex, no violence. Why would anyone read it? We then kept going to publishers for another couple of months. It was rejected by another 22 publishers, and then our agent said, 'Sorry boys, I can't sell it.'" We all know what happened next!

Richard Bach's *Jonathan Livingston Seagull* was rejected and turned down 140 times. J. K. Rowling's original work was turned away by 12 publishers. Imagine rejecting *Harry Potter*! I bet they are sorry for not taking a chance on then–single mother J. K. Rowling!

Rejection is not a new thing. Margaret Mitchell's *Gone With the Wind* was rejected 38 times, and *Carrie* by Stephen King was turned down 30 times. Finally, what is now considered a masterpiece, E. E. Cummings' first work, *The Enormous Room*, was rejected so many times that it was ultimately self-published, dedicated to the publishers who rejected it. (You've got to love that one!) If you need more evidence of rejection, visit this site; you'll be surprised how many pushed through.

www.OneHundredRejections.com

When you look at the numbers, the only thing that can stop you from putting your work out there is your own fear of doing it. With this book, you will have the strategy, the tools, and the will to get it done, remember to just play it like a game. Let me remind you again that when you put a book out there, you are a published author in a space where you are an expert. Your book becomes the ultimate business card, not to mention a source of ongoing revenue.

Did someone say "ongoing revenue?" Who doesn't need to make some extra money on a regular basis? Realize that this book will take some work to complete, but after that it exists forever—bringing you royalty checks 5, 10, 20 years from now. Money will be consistently flowing into your bank account. If you write a good book that provides real value, then you realistically have a revenue stream, which will bring income for decades to come.

PERFECTION

Have no fear of perfection—you'll never reach it.

▶ *Salvador Dali*

No one is asking you to write the masterpiece of all books. Nor do you need to sell a million copies to be successful. You simply need to own and present an interesting idea to like-minded people. For many, that will open doors that will enable them to seize the right opportunities. For others, their interest in a particular subject will generate enough book sales to bring in revenue.

If you are waiting for the time for your information to be perfect, then let me give you some advice: That time will never come. The time to write your book is *now*! Something motivated you to buy this book about doing just that, so use this energy to focus on the clear benefits to you and your family and surrender the wish to be perfect. Just play the game, a little every day.

> I am careful not to confuse excellence with perfection. Excellence, I can reach for; perfection is God's business.
>
> ▶ *Michael J. Fox*

Do your best, and do it now!

FUTURE PLANNING

Imagine for a moment the profound and life-changing effects of sharing this information with your family, especially your children. What would happen if you challenged your children to share their interests by writing a book? What if you took it a step beyond and taught them how to do this entire process, all while playing this game? Imagine beginning to do this and creating a new mission each year. Theoretically, by high school graduation, your child may have several bestsellers and a business in place. Remember that each one is structured in a way for them to earn passive income.

In a previous chapter I shared that I am a homeschooling parent. I do this process twice a year, and as a result, my children have created several websites, books, and products. These require minimal maintenance yet keep a steady flow of income to their bank accounts. My children do not need to beg me for an allowance because they make their own money. They are allowed to purchase what they want and usually re-invest in themselves by adding domain names, buying software to make their work easier or more streamlined, and researching live events they want to attend.

When we attend these events, they are completely focused on the speakers and are taking notes. When we return home, they are inspired to immediately implement and test the new things they have learned. Some ideas work well, while others do not. This teaches them that mistakes or failures are okay; they are just a part of the process. When they discover what works, they move forward quickly and with determination to master what they have just implemented. They know that the time and attention they invest is ultimately for their future, and they are excited to be building that future themselves.

As a parent, I know that the lessons they learn by doing are an invaluable asset for their adult lives. The natural byproduct of this process is that they are responsible, not afraid of trying new things, enjoy challenges, and have self-confidence. They respect entrepreneurs because they know their process. Their creativity is supported and encouraged as they learn to "think outside the box" by building new things. They speak with confidence and certainty because they have been through the processes from start to finish.

Whether or not you decide to follow my example with your own children, you will have a solid source of passive income that continues to appear in your account long after your first book is done. Consider doing this each year (or a few times per year) to set several channels in place. You will be building a reliable nest egg for your family's future.

MISSION COMMAND

Congratulations!

You have completed the initiation process and are now in "game mode."

Welcome to Mission Command.

Mission Command is where you will be introduced to the overall strategy of the game. It is your gateway to the Intelligence Sector, where you will become more aware of the tools that are available to you. More importantly, you will understand how to coordinate these tools in a strategic manner to best serve your mission.

INTELLIGENCE SECTOR

This is the Intelligence Sector, where you will be assigned numerous operations. Your goal is to complete each operation with a deeper knowledge and understanding. This will enable you to properly use the information after your primary mission is complete.

Intelligence Sector Overview:

OPERATION: Construct
Platform

OPERATION: Credibility
Performance

OPERATION: Create
Publishing

OPERATION: Captivate
Positioning

OPERATION: Capture
Branding

OPERATION: Connect
Social Media

OPERATION: Convert
Sales

OPERATION: CONSTRUCT

THE PLATFORM

Everything you do from here on in needs to come from a home base. For this mission, your website is your home base. It does not matter if you have a business or a service, whether you work in your office or from home. Without a home base on the Internet, you are not prepared for global access and you are tragically limiting your reach.

Research, experience, and results have continuously pointed me towards using WordPress as my own hosting account. In this operation you need to secure the following:

- Domain name (your www.yourname.com address)
- Website hosting
- WordPress (WordPress.org, not the WordPress.com free site)
- A WordPress theme that works for your author page (I recommend BrandingTheme.com.)
- An auto-responder service to build your list and create an opt-in box
- A PayPal account for accepting payments online

Different authors have different kinds of websites, but the goal is to keep it very simple. For your convenience, I have created a page with the tools and providers I use. You may access it here:

www.BeMoreThanYouAre.com/free-tools

If you already have a website as part of your existing business, I still recommend getting a separate site highlighting your book and yourself as an author. Consider getting a custom and unique URL (www.yourbookname.com) for the book name.

On your specific author site you will need to create the following pages:

- Home page (where visitors arrive)
- Author page (about you)
- Book page (specific to your book)
- Events page (for your book-signing or speaking calendar)
- Media page (your interviews, news stories, and press)
- Contact page (where you can be contacted)
- Blog or news page (if you wish to post regularly, and I recommend you do!)

These are the bare-bones minimum pages you need to begin. WordPress themes come with a sidebar area where you can place your "widgets." Widgets are little place markers where you can put a string of code to connect to your other sites and services (like social media and sign-up forms). Widgets can also hold code for any audio or video you wish to share.

The mission of the Intelligence Sector is to give you a general understanding of the working pieces of each operation and to help you write a book that ties it all together for the greatest result. I do have a complete program that walks you through each operation in greater depth, which you can learn about here:

www.BeMoreThanYouAre.com/training

The purpose of the training is to show you how to leverage your expertise so you can expand your revenue and freedom through passive income–producing products and services. It is important to stack the necessary building blocks to grow a business that will flourish, continue to grow, and stand the test of time.

There are two very important things you must share on your author page. The first is your image, and the second is the cover of your book(s). You may put some quotes from the book on your author page. It is also important to place some endorsements or reviews on the site. Include a link for editors or other media people to be able to get complimentary review copies.

Your media page should have the same link as well, along with several professional photographs of you and your book cover for editorials and reviews. The easier you make this for the media, the better your chances will be for being professionally reviewed and interviewed.

There are author site services, but you can also do it yourself. The training program I mention above walks you through each step.

There are many website designers who cater primarily to authors. One such provider is AuthorsOnTheWeb.com. They use language the layperson does not understand to make the idea of site building difficult.

> We build our sites' content management systems (CMS) so that authors who wish to have the capacity to update their websites on their own, independent of having our team make their updates, can do so.
>
> ▶ *AuthorsOnTheWeb*

This simply means they are building their authors' sites on a Word-Press blog platform. The same one you can download very quickly and easily.

The last time I checked their site, their prices started at $3,800, and if you want them to manage it for you, it jumped to $5500. If you are willing to do it yourself, your investment will be closer to $200 for your domain, hosting, and a theme.

You can choose to learn WordPress on your own or invest in training. There are literally hundreds of WordPress courses given daily throughout the country, and you're sure to find one near you quite easily. If you do not wish to invest time in learning WordPress for yourself, my team also offers a "done for you" author website package with a much better pricing structure than what you saw above:

www.BeMoreThanYouAre.com/author-site-done-for-you

A great thing about WordPress is that changes are instant and made by you; you never have to be held hostage by your webmaster again. But perhaps the greatest benefit is that it seamlessly synchronizes with social media, and that is very powerful.

WordPress also aligns with your auto-responder. This is called your "opt-in" and is where visitors give you their name and email address so you can continue to communicate with them via email to announce your book-signing events, speaking engagements, etc. In this process visitors gives you their name and email address in exchange for a small gift, such as a chapter from your book. This is your start to building a valuable email list of people interested in your subject matter. If you have an award or special recognition, you can put that on your site as well.

I suggest browsing through and finding websites that you like. If you have favorite authors, you could look and see how their sites are laid out and designed. Your design should convey your personal brand in a way that complements both you and your book.

Another thing you can do with WordPress is to create a direct link to your CreateSpace store for bulk book ordering. (You will learn more about this in a later mission.) Additionally, you get the highest royalties when books sell directly from the store. Remember to always include a link to your bookstore on CreateSpace or other platform.

All authors need a powerful platform that serves as their home base, and WordPress is ideally suited to make it as easy as can be, with you fully in control. The ease with which your site can be maintained allows you to sell more books, help more people, and make more money.

OPERATION: CREDIBILITY

PERFORMANCE

Let's talk about the benefits of your performance as an expert. I am a great believer in furthering your education and am constantly attending conferences, symposiums, and workshops given by experts in fields I am interested in learning more about. This has allowed me to actually learn from the top people in the field and to network with like-minded people and the leaders themselves. I get to see them "perform" in the area of their expertise, and this is invaluable in learning how to position myself in fields I'm interested in.

Although many of these events are pricey, they are also "priceless" for staying up to date on the current trends, the latest technologies, and what is relevant today. But the greatest values are in the relationships built at such events and in studying how the experts communicate and build rapport with their audience.

What is it worth to have one-on-one time with thought leaders and experts, to have access to the people who are leading the field in their areas of expertise? I cannot convey the mega value of sitting down with Anthony Robbins, spending a week in Hawaii with people like Lisa Nichols, Gay Hendricks, Lynne Twist, Yanik Silver, Arielle Ford, Burt Goldman, and Vishen Lakhiani, or the value of watching my daughter post pictures together with her new friend Brendon Burchard.

Aligning with mentors and experts is not only good for your growth to continue to be the very best you can be, but it also helps you to raise the bar for yourself and aspire to grow so you better serve your customers.

You will notice that throughout this book I will recommend various experts and their products. Pay close attention, as I do not do this lightly. The core lesson is that if you learn from the best, you will be the best!

> Tell me and I forget, teach me and I may remember, involve me and I learn.
>
> ▶ *Benjamin Franklin*

When using the word "expert," the best place to begin is with Brendon Burchard's books *The Charge* and *The Millionaire Messenger*. Brendon has literally written the books on how to become the expert in your chosen space and position yourself for success.

Burchard's "Expert's Academy" is the most respected training available. If you are not familiar with Brendon and his work, I invite you to learn more:

BeMoreThanYouAre.com/Brendon

ALIGNMENT

When I speak of alignment, I mean aligning yourself with current leaders in your niche or field. As a whole, when you stand alongside those with respect and credibility and are seen and heard in the same space, a certain amount of respect carries over to you.

Alignment means sharing those photos taken with your favorite guru when you share the article you've written about the experience. It provides social authority and third-party validation. It allows people see you in greater company, company worth keeping.

We consider alignment each time we go to a new restaurant, buy a product, or see a film. We read the reviews, we see how it is rated and what others are saying, and often our decision to try something new comes as a direct result of what we have read, seen, or heard. We feel safer because risk is reduced and our decision becomes easier to make.

Use alignment to your advantage, whether in your branding, positioning, or launching of a new product. The more aligned you are, the stronger your message or unique proposal can be. Alignment helps get you the credibility and visibility you need. This is especially true when authoring a book.

ENDORSEMENTS

When writing your book, think about the fellow experts you mention, interview, or discuss. Who are the current leading authorities in your field? Create a plan of action to contact them and ask for their endorsement.

The formula that has worked for me has three important steps:

Create Awesome Content.
Whether it is your book, coaching package, or "how-to system," make sure it is something they will be comfortable associating their name with. Set your standards high, and deliver only the best work possible. If they see examples of your unique personality and experience combined with a quality product, they will be more likely to come on board.

Create a "Who's Who" List and Ask Them All.
My list always begins with 50 people. My formula is to contact the first 10 and wait a couple of days. If one comes in, I use it to leverage the new letters I send. Do not allow yourself to be intimidated or shy about approaching them; after all, you are on your way to dominating your space, too. Never assume they will say no and not send it; shoot for the sky! Many people fail simply by not trying. What is the worst that can happen: They will say no? Remember, you have numerous others. Keep going for yes.

Ask The Question, and Direct Response.
Experts tend to be busy and hyper-organized. They want to help you, but the easier you make it for them, the better. They most

likely do not have time to read your entire book or try out your 12-hour course, so summarize and highlight the strong points for them. Give them specific guidelines to make it very easy on their part. I always include a very brief sample with a description. I write this out passionately and always focus on why I created the product (whom I want to help, how this information will make others' lives easier, etc.). I offer to send them the entire product but also write that I understand they are very busy and that 2–3 sentences is all I am looking for. If I already have another endorsement, I include it in the form of "By the way, Expert Guru said it was . . ." (and I insert the quote from expert guru).

I let them know packaging is set to go to print, and I need it by a specific deadline. In my experience, one week works best. If they get it a few days late from their assistants, even better, because now they can review it, write their piece, and send. Remember, they want to help you; they are usually just very busy.

My endorsement request for this book was worded in this manner:

I have written a book *Book Power: A Platform for Writing, Branding, Positioning, & Publishing*. The book will be going to print on March 1, so that is my deadline. I have also created a full coaching back-end product walking students through everything I teach in the book. I will be happy to get you more information because I'd love a written endorsement from you as well as your consideration on becoming an affiliate for the coaching product.

The book goes in depth on how to write a book quickly by using my gamified process. Additionally, it shows how to properly brand yourself, position yourself, align social media, and build a platform for overall success.

I can send you the cover design and a PDF of the book if you need.

If you're willing to help (no pressure if you can't) just reply with "Sure, I'll help" and then either send your endorsement to kytka@ bemorethanyouare.com before March 1st or ask a question or two and I'll send more info. This shouldn't take more than 10 minutes out of your busy day and will help us get more people involved in writing their own book to share their special messages adding value to the world. Below are some endorsements I have already received.

I would love to have your input for the book and look forward to your reply. Thanks so much in advance for your help!

Do not take it personally if you do not get everyone to endorse you. For all you know they are hanging out with Richard Branson on Nekker Island this week!

Of course when one comes in, you will want to update your letter to include some of the new endorsements, hence the reason I always send a handful first and then wait a few days before I send out the bulk.

Make sure to follow up immediately with a thank you. Keep it short, but make sure they know you appreciate what they just did for you. If you were asking for a book endorsement, remember to send them a signed copy on publication.

Finally, use the endorsement in your marketing and art for your finished product. You will notice that the back covers of most bestselling books no longer have book descriptions but rather a list of powerful endorsements. And don't forget to blast out to your social media followers because getting respect from a fellow expert is a visibility tool that elevates your own reputation. There is plenty of room at the top!

You are on your way!

OPERATION: CREATE

CHOICE TO SELF-PUBLISH

Self publishing has exploded. According to a recent survey, 81 percent of people feel that they have a book in them . . . and should write it.

▶ *New York Times*

If you do the math, that represents over 200 million people in the United States who want to write a book in their lifetime!

There is a new concept, "wag the long tail," which means if you rack up enough small sales, especially consumer sales on the Internet, it will add up to big profits in the long run. Technology is turning mass markets into millions of niches. Independent presses, self-publishers, and authors can sell effectively into these micromarkets. This bodes well for new and mid-list authors, not to mention creative-minded smaller presses.

Balboa Press summarized this trend best when they said, "First there were independent films. Then music listeners wanted to make their own music under their own labels, and we had independent music. But what about authors? They were left with difficult do-it-yourself publishing or vanity presses that didn't give the professional edge most authors were looking for. Fortunately, technology caught up with what authors were looking for and produced assisted self-publishing using print-on-demand technology. Now, the way books are published and get into the marketplace is changing. E-books are becoming more popular and traditional publishing houses are scrambling to make a profit on their books."

Maybe you have already been writing but never considered a book before. What you have contributed to websites, discussion groups, blogs, and membership communities can lead to books. These are great places to flesh out ideas, get reader feedback, and sometimes even catch the attention of an agent, publisher, or larger audience. If anything, a well-branded presence on the Internet positions you in a way where you have the opportunity to become the authority or expert. Do not let any of what you have written online go to waste. Make files and collect all of your information because you may have enough content already written to fill two books!

Once again, my personal preferred self-publishing ally is Amazon's CreateSpace and Kindle Direct Publishing (KDP), so I will refer to them throughout this book. They have always served me well, and I have assisted numerous others in self publishing with them.

Let me share my first self-publishing journey with you. Back in the days before CreateSpace, I self-published my first book. The year was 1997; my son had a question about something new he was learning, and I referred him to look for a book on the subject. At the time, there were no books on the subject, and my son asked me to help gather some information for him to study. As I began to research and find facts, I discovered that the language was difficult, the information too mature. So I began writing my own version of what I had researched to make it more palatable and interesting for my son. About 10 days later, I had written my first book.

Perhaps it came out of me easily because I wanted to provide the information to my son in a fun, exciting, and understandable way. Perhaps in using this approach, I did not set myself up for writer's block or inner talk telling me I was not a writer. Whatever the case, I wrote a book in 10 days. Now here is the best part: I am still making money from that book over 15 years later. I have also since written numerous other books that I still get paid from to this very day.

It is difficult to express the joy I feel each month when the royalty check comes. I can only tell you that it feels wonderful to know that I dedicated some time and focus to create something that helps people, and for that effort, I still collect earnings every month. I do not need to worry about basic expenses any longer, no matter what happens, because I know that those royalties will continue to roll in each month. I keep sneaking this in because I want you to experience the freedom of having a residual income too!

My books are not #1 bestsellers nor did I expect them to be. They did reach #2 and #5 when I was testing some promotional strategies, but that comes later. Your book does not need to be a bestseller to make a nice income. My books share valuable information, which I gathered and learned along my path and that other people find interesting, informative, and, more importantly, useful.

In life, we are all on the same journey, we are all struggling to get from point A to point B. Different people have different point A originations and B destinations, but the path we travel is the same.

If you can take what you have learned, share the experience and shortcuts you've discovered along the way, and offer time-saving tips and how you finally made it, then you can lighten the load of those who are just beginning on a similar path. Getting paid for it is an added bonus.

My hope is that you do not end your journey at "I wrote a book," but rather understand that your book is just the beginning. Imagine the products you can create based on the contents of your book. Imagine the opportunities to share your knowledge with more people by speaking, training, and coaching. You have an important message to share and the world is waiting . . .

OPERATION: CAPTIVATE

POSITIONING

The results of positioning yourself as an author/expert are increased visibility, growth of communities of loyal brand enthusiasts, increased profits, and greater overall success for your business.

Now we need to discuss the importance of strategy for positioning you, your products and services, or your company for success.

Position is a simple, credible story that can be summarized in one or two keywords or phrases. It is about owning or dominating your idea in your niche or market space. The most successful and recognized companies have strong business positioning. Some powerful examples of this would be Apple owning "smartphones," Nike owning "performance," and well, Pfizer owning "Viagra = performance." All of these illustrate this idea. For your business or product to succeed, you need a winning/dominant position to showcase your brand.

When defining your position, match your business strategy with one of the following methods and shape it to fit your unique style, business philosophy, or product characteristics. Then, launch your idea into the market space and carve out your niche.

To own or dominate your niche, your goal is to attract those customers from your biggest competitor by becoming the local expert in that niche/space. You cannot be defeated if you are known as the local expert. The more knowledgeable and passionate you are about your business, the more customers you will gain from the "other guy." Never try to accomplish this by competing on price; rather, focus on rising above the competition by concentrating on these areas:

- Share your expert advice.
- Nurture your personal relationships.
- Engage your customers.
- Build quality products.
- Deliver consistent value.
- Communicate with integrity.
- Guarantee excellent service.
- Offer strong customer support.
- Lead by staying abreast of new trends.
- Over-deliver on your promise.

Doing the above will create strong attachments with your following and will bring repeat clients.

Build a service, product, or shopping experience so great the people will have no choice except to say "Wow!" each time they think of you. Give them the little extras that they can't find anywhere else! Go beyond expectations when it comes to service, and include an element of pleasant surprise every now and again to keep it interesting. Over time, this will result in repeat business, word-of-mouth recommendations (which are always best) from satisfied customers, and true brand loyalty.

OPERATION: CAPTURE

BRANDING

Your brand is the unique persona and identity of you, your company, product, or service that sets it apart from others in the same market space. It is the image you or your business present to the world. A brand is composed of many different pieces which together capture the attention of your buyers. Some of the pieces are physical, but much of branding is intangible; ideas and thoughts put into words, pictures, and videos. When small business owners ask themselves, "What is branding?" the answer is, "The essence of the business, products, or services."

Your personal brand conveys the way you are perceived and how you want people to see and feel about you, your business, and your products or services. You may want to sound very dignified and reinforce your expert status and credibility, depending on your products or services. Or you may want to sound approachable, edgy, and smart. Whatever voice you choose, carry it into all your messaging, marketing materials, and web presence (your platform).

The words and images you communicate position you or your company in the market space. Anything you write about your company should do at least two of these six things:

- Differentiate yourself from others in your space.
- Offer a benefit.
- Reinforce your brand.
- Reinforce your expert status.
- Build authority and credibility.
- Show alignment with other experts in your niche.

Let's take a quick look at the best brand and most valuable company by market valuation in the world. That's right, it's Apple. Not only are their products, computers, iPads, and iPhones cutting-edge and outperforming the competition, they are absolutely beautiful in design! I invite you to visit an Apple store not only to look at the world's best branding job but also to take a look at how they are packaged for the consumer. Their color is white, and the boxes are custom made with the most incredible white cardboard which fits their products like a glove. If you had to follow a "branding pattern," this would be the one to emulate.

Make the best product you can, pleasing to all of the senses, and package it in the same manner! Hanover Printing says, "Branding is very much like a system; think of it as your Quickbooks or Excel, but for your visual database," and I agree. Your brand needs to be a well-planned and organized system to give your viewers and potential customers a consistent image of you and your products, services, or company. Branding occurs every time you do something concerning your products or company. The list is endless, but here is the beginning:

- Email: Signature, Logo, and Colors
- Regular Mail: Stationery and Envelopes
- Business Cards
- Infographics and Memes
- Websites and Banners
- Packaging Materials (Remember Apple!)
- Newsletters

- Handouts for live events
- Advertisements
- Blogs
- Social media

Keep in mind that in today's world your potential client is looking online to see who you are. Keeping all of your branding consistent gives them a feeling of security and builds trust. It shows your organization, personality, and that you take care to present yourself in a well-aligned manner. This is the sign of professionalism, which is imperative to doing business in today's social landscape. Keep your Facebook, Twitter, YouTube, Pinterest, LinkedIn, and other sites up to date with any major changes to branding.

Liz Goodgold of Redfire Branding sums it up best when she says, "To be successful, you must own your brand. Make it small enough to own and large enough to grow." With that in mind, understand that most people choose the term "trustworthy" as the most important brand personality attribute when discussing their favorite brands. This is because the brand takes on a life and personality of its own. Buying decisions are made on a certain expectation based on trust.

Therefore, spend time to consider ways you can maintain consistency across following:

- Consistent presentation across the board
- Consistent level of quality
- Consistent level of service
- Consistent communication style
- Consistent product functionality or features
- Consistent product availability
- Consistent reliability levels
- Consistent time delivery
- Consistent performance

Remember, your customers are counting on your brand to appear aligned with your message. Be consistent and predictable when it comes to branding.

Now that you have the idea of how important branding is to the ultimate success of your products, services, and company, I urge you do further reading on the subject. I have included a section on branding in the recommended reading section.

OPERATION: CONNECT

SOCIAL MEDIA

With the explosion of technology over the last 15+ years, we are in the process of a complete paradigm shift with regard to how we communicate in our marketing, public relations, and advertising. Social media has forever changed the way businesses and customers communicate, and the beauty of it is that, through your channels, you can reach your audience directly and at lightning speed. Social media have also changed the way customers make their buying decisions. Pinterest, Google+, Twitter, YouTube, and Facebook have made it easy to find and connect with others who share similar interests, to read product reviews, and to connect with potential clients. Within these networks there is an amazing and wide-open space for your unique voice to be heard. As the web interacts with us in more personal ways and with greater portability, there is no time better than the present to engage with and rally your community.

The buzzword in today's marketing is all about "engaging in meaningful conversations." These conversations take place when you communicate on your blog, through your website, and on your social media channels in a way that invites response from your following. Such conversations are the foundations of strong relationships, and in those relationships, trust is formed. Invite your following to communicate with you and deliver value consistently. They will come to know you as the expert, and they will not only follow you, but share and recommend you to others.

When Facebook first came on to the scene, people believed it would appeal only to the college crowd it was designed for, but we all quickly jumped on board. Now Facebook is accepted as an important business tool to engage your brand with your community. Twitter followed suit with making communication fast and instant with 140-character tweets, and finally Pinterest came into being, where now we can convey our message with just an image.

Having these accounts linked creates an advertising team working for you around the clock. The idea is to keep yourself in front of the crowd.

MISSION: Cross-Pollination

Cross-pollination between sites is always a good way to increase people's loyalty to your brand.

Today's writers need to incorporate social media into their marketing strategy. Keeping a blog or a newsletter and developing a personal relationship with your readers is a bonus. Do not try to work with all of the social media sites or you will find yourself with no time to write your book! Stick to the big five: Facebook, Twitter, YouTube, Pinterest, and Google+, and you will be able to reach 90% of the market.

MISSION: Social Media Optimization (SMO)

As you begin to understand how social media works, recognize that your most important mission is to understand how it works together. When you plan your marketing strategies, focus not only on SEO (search engine optimization) but also on SMO (social media optimization).

Wikipedia defines SMO this way: "Social media optimization (SMO) refers to the use of a number of social media outlets and communities to generate publicity to increase the awareness of a product, brand or event."

Bingo. "Generate *publicity* to *increase the awareness* of a product, *brand* or event." That sentence alone is reason enough to pay attention to social media.

Wikipedia continues: "Social media optimization is becoming increasingly important for search engine optimization, as search engines are increasingly utilizing the recommendations of users of social networks such as Facebook, Twitter, and Google+ to rank pages in the search engine result pages. The implication is that when a webpage is shared or 'liked' by a user on a social network, it counts as a 'vote' for that webpage's quality. Thus, search engines can use such votes accordingly to properly rank websites in search engine results pages. Furthermore, since it is more difficult to tip the scales or influence the search engines in this way, search engines are putting more stock into 'social search.'"

OPERATION: CONVERT

SALES

If we could sell our experiences for what they cost us, we'd all be millionaires.

▶ *Abigail Van Buren*

The most effective sales people are those who are truly authentic and passionate about what they are selling. If you have created something that makes people's lives easier, then all you need to do is inform them about your product. If it is any good, it will sell itself. The trick is to keep it in front of them and not let it, or you, get buried at the bottom of the pile. Henry Ford said, "The man who will use his skill and constructive imagination to see how much he can give for a dollar, instead of how little he can give for a dollar, is bound to succeed." Wonderful advice.

When you read books about sales and marketing, you will learn about something referred to as "touches." Touches are the number of times you make contact with a customer before a sale is made. Social media makes touches happen all of the time, and the quality of your touches is directly related to your brand. Most experts agree that, on average, seven touches are necessary. In *Rule of Seven*, Dr.

Jeffrey Lant states, "You must contact your buyers a minimum of seven times in an 18-month period for them to remember you." Of course, most of Jeffrey's books were written in the '90s, when social media had not yet been born.

Wikipedia states: "Related to the idea of multi-touch leads is the 'Seven Contact to Sale Theory,' which delivers leads that start with an outbound call, followed by an email and sometimes postal piece. By the time the lead purchaser gets the lead, the customer is familiar with their brand and has an opportunity to request additional information."

Jay Abraham, known as the "$9.4 Billion Dollar Man," states seven as the number of times you interact with a customer asking for a sale before you get a yes.

> It is not your customer's job to remember you. It is your obligation and responsibility to make sure they don't have the chance to forget you.
>
> ▶ *Patricia Fripp*

You must structure your touches for the best effect for selling while maintaining your stance as the valued expert who is teaching and sharing. Make sure that all products you create give your audience the opportunity to make an educated buying decision. Answer their questions before they ask them. What I mean by this is to identify the problem and then share how your product gives the solution to the problem. Give evidence of your product having worked through testimonials and endorsements from people who have seen the difference you are making. Map it out for them so they have an idea of what they must do before beginning, how long it should take them, and where they will be at the end. What should they expect in terms of results? How long will it take for them to see results? The more information you give up front, the more confident your customer will feel. If questions arise, create an FAQ page and answer each one. Straighten out any misconceptions, and do not allow room for confusion. When you have a product page that answers all questions, you are more likely to convert people into customers.

> Selling is getting someone intellectually engaged in a future result that is good for them and getting them to emotionally commit to take action to achieve that result.
>
> ▸ *Dan Sullivan, Modern Marketing Column at Success.com*

I first came across the above quote through Joe Polish of Piranha Marketing, and it really does sum it up in the very best way. Joe has created a wonderful video animation that is one of the best lessons in sales I've seen. It is short and effective, and I encourage you to take the four minutes to watch:

http://www.youtube.com/watch?v=e2ZXAhV8lzg

Selling is crucial to your success because without the sale you do not make any money. The great thing about writing a book to position yourself is that the book does a lot of the selling for you. People can read the book and come to you for more answers. If you have products created to match the theme of your book, your platform (website) will do the selling for you. Automate as much of the process as you can with opt-in boxes, video sales landing pages, and special offers.

Make it as easy as you can for your fans and followers. Once your products are created, simply write about them, talk about them, create articles from the content, and say yes to interviews. The buzz created will point people back to your site, where your automatic sales team is ready to take orders 24 hours a day.

Sales Funnels

I learned about effective sales funnels from Yanik Silver. Yanik is a serial Internet entrepreneur and self-made millionaire. He is recognized as one of the leading experts worldwide on web marketing. He is respected and well liked in the entrepreneurial space and has a goal to get 10,000 young entrepreneurs aged 13–23 to start their own companies by the year 2020. I met Yanik in Hawaii at an event called *Awesomeness Fest* and as a result began paying closer attention to what he does online.

Last year my children Zynnia and Zachary were invited to his event *Underground 8*, and they came home with an amazing DVD where Yanik shared a powerful strategy for his back-end sales funnel. In one instant, everything crystallized and made sense. Seeing that video was a game changer for me, and I share this with you here because I want to stress again that we are always learning.

Mentors are such an important part of keeping up to date on your journey and one of the best ways to remain on top. Spending time with thought leaders and other entrepreneurs gives you an edge that most people lack. Not only does it align you with experts, but it has this wonderful side effect of bringing out the very best in you. We are the company we keep, and the more you hang out with successful people, the more successful you will be.

Writing your book is not the "be all end all" of your strategy, but it is a powerful catalyst that can push you to the top of your game. You see, something magical happens when you write your book, and this is the best place to mention it, because a sale happens when your book is complete. You sell yourself on the idea that you are more than you previously believed yourself to be. You get to experience that "I did it" moment where your mind releases these wonderful stimulators that make you feel awesome. You see yourself in a different way, and this opens up a greater opportunity for accomplishment, achievement, and success.

So seek out your heroes in your niche or field. Find out where they are and go hang out with them. You'll be surprised at how nice and receptive they are once they see you are seriously committed to your own growth while building your business and growing your platform.

Locate the people who have influenced you, mentored you, inspired you, and challenged you to grow yourself, your brand, and your business. After your book is published, consider aligning with these heroes to collaborate and build both of your platforms in a positive way.

Most people are unaware of what goes on in a sales funnel sequence. In the beginning you have unqualified prospects who have been introduced to your site. The best way to capture these prospects is to have an opt-in form where they can sign up. I recommend offering a special gift in exchange for their contact information. The next step would be to offer initial communication in the form of an email and asking for response. You want to begin a discussion with your prospect. In your response, you show that you have developed a solution and you present that solution to them in the form of sending them to your sales page. Ideally, your sales page has a video where you discuss the solution and benefits and offer a call to action. The prospect can then either purchase the solution or leave the page.

In the strategy I learned from Yanik, you present an offer to buy a low-entry product. The customer initiates a purchase and is in the checkout or shopping cart process. Instead of sending them directly to the order page, you send them to another higher-priced offer, which is normally sold for more on your site. In other words, they receive an opportunity to get a "big ticket" item at reduced cost. Yanik shares that up to 66% of people will take the special offer. Now they have an option to say yes or no to the second offer. Whether they say yes or no, they are again given an offer for an upsell on the order page (introducing a third product offer). He shares that another 15% will take this upsell (whether or not they took the second offer).

Most people are unaware of these back-side funnel strategies, and yet Internet marketing experts use them all of the time. If you look at the numbers, 66% and 15% conversions can have a massive impact on your sales. Finally, you can also present one more offer on the thank-you page. For example, if you have a private members' area or newsletter, you may offer to sign them up for a three-month free trial with an auto-billing option that takes effect after 90 days. If you provide value on a consistent basis, they will not cancel after the 90 days because they are accustomed to receiving the benefits for your members' access or newsletter.

The overall strategy Yanik and others have mastered is to get customers into the order cart sequence and that is where they do most of their selling, whereas most people set out to sell just one item, take their customer to the cart, and complete one transaction. Those with a limited view of the sale do not understand the power and advantage of having customers in the order cart when presenting one-time offers, which again, 66% of customers will purchase.

An example of this funnel sequence for you as an author would look like this: Your book which sells for $18.95 can be offered to your clients free with a nominal charge for shipping ($6.95). Let's say the cost of your book is $2.80 and to mail it is $2.65 first-class mail. You have made $1.50 profit on a "lead," which is now in your shopping cart. If you follow the strategy above, you could send them to a webinar you have prerecorded (selling for $47), which guides them through the processes outlined in your book. You could sell them a training program (selling for $147) in which you allow them to look over your shoulder as you walk them through the steps in your book, etc. If 66% take the first offer for a $47 up sell, that means 66% of your leads purchased on a lead that you made money on. In traditional pay-per-click marketing, you would normally have to pay for those leads, but here you make the $1.50 with a 66% chance of making an additional $47 and a 15% chance of making an additional $147. Finally, on the thank-you page, you offer membership free for 90 days, but then they are billed $17 monthly. Do you understand how these numbers begin to add up? And again, most people wonder how experts and gurus make any money giving away their books for free. The key to an effective sales funnel strategy is that you have all of the pieces in place before you launch and take them through the checkout process because that is where most sales occur.

Aligned Selling and Cross-Marketing

Today's games are played in the spirit of cooperation and collaboration rather than competitiveness. The best models are ones where you see a win–win–win. The customer wins for having the greatest information; the creator wins for being accountable to build the best content; and the collaborator wins for being a part of something that makes the world a better place. You see, I believe that our legacy is to leave behind the information we have gathered on our journey and to share it in order to make another's journey easier. I'm sure you have seen websites announcing books or events where you can see not one or two, but a dozen or more of your favorite gurus. These folks are working together in an aligned manner to grow all of their individual businesses.

Can you identify the right networks, people, keywords, influencers, or communities that align with what you are doing? What would be an ideal win–win situation for you both? Perhaps you could fill a gap they have or vice versa. Develop products in your space that are complementary to and not in competition with those of the mentors and thought leaders that you admire. In this way, you have simplified the approach to cross-marketing!

GAME PLAN

LEVELS

Levels are composed of several missions that can be completed in any order, but it is better to complete them sequentially, as completing an earlier mission will make later ones easier. Do not worry about the end result during this process, and do not allow yourself to become distracted or sidetracked. Focus on completing each mission before you go to the next level.

So are you ready to play a much bigger game? Are you prepared to challenge yourself to take the steps necessary to write your book? I believe you are because you know your future depends on it.

To play you will need the following:

Shopping List
- Index cards
- File folders

Recon
- Trip to bookstore
- Trip to library
- Amazon spy games
- Make sure to visit the bonus pages at BeMoreThanYouAre. com for your gifts from this book.

Collecting Mission Bonuses

- Visit BeMoreThanYouAre.com secret locations to collect bonuses mentioned within the mission.

You will progress through various levels, and in each level you will be given specific missions. Begin at Level One and do not move on to Level Two until all of the missions are complete.

As you pass through each level, keep your overall strategy in mind. Did you have a grandparent who sometimes said, "Mind your Ps and Qs"? For the sake of our mission, I want you to embed this command into your memory:

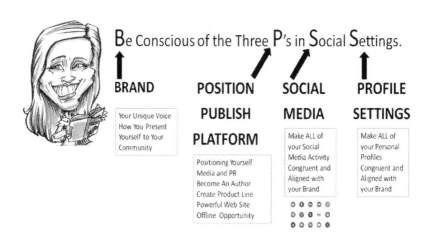

Be Conscious of the Three P's in Social Settings.

BRAND
Your Unique Voice
How You Present
Yourself to Your
Community

POSITION
PUBLISH
PLATFORM
Positioning Yourself
Media and PR
Become An Author
Create Product Line
Powerful Web Site
Offline Opportunity

SOCIAL
MEDIA
Make ALL of
your Social
Media Activity
Congruent and
Aligned with
your Brand

PROFILE
SETTINGS
Make ALL of
your Personal
Profiles
Congruent and
Aligned with
your Brand

LEVEL ONE

MISSION: THE TITLE

The best place to begin is to create a title for your book. Take the time to really give this some thought. "What kind of a title?" you may be asking. Well, first off, let go of that magical book title that you've been imagining because people most likely are not aligned in the same way that you might be thinking.

The best titles are one-, two-, or three-word titles that basically answer the need or the problem of your audience. For example, if your audience is saying, "I don't understand social media" or "I am so confused about the difference between Facebook and Twitter," then your title should be *Social Media Explained* or *Understanding Social Media*. The best titles convey meaning elegantly and also describe the benefit.

Always look at the question or the problem of your client, your audience, and your ideal target customer (market), and then focus on the primary question they are asking.

In her book *Creative Nonfiction*, author Eileen Pollack suggests that before writing you ought to select a topic and then pose a question. She suggests that a question creates a focus and purpose for writing.

For instance, suppose you recall a memory and ask yourself: What is so important about this memory? What did I learn from the personal experience? Why is it significant? Is there a universal truth? Or suppose you wanted to write a meditative essay on freedom. You could start by posing a question to yourself: What is freedom to me?

The shortest possible answer to your primary question is the title of your book, which most likely will be perfect. Be specific and never vague. Avoid buzzwords, numbers, text talk, initials, and spelling shortcuts. *Social Media 4 You* is probably not the best title for your book.

Additionally, you need to consider something that Amazon refers to as relevance in their search engine. I have included a chapter called "Getting It Right The First Time" where I go much deeper into this, so I suggest you read that chapter as well before deciding upon your title.

You will also want to go into a bookstore and browse through the titles in the nonfiction bestseller section of motivational, DIY (do it yourself), personal development, marketing, self-help, and how-to books. Publishing companies hire high-priced consultants to come up with a powerful title, or "headline," because book publishing is big business; therefore a lot of thought goes into making their titles as commercially viable as possible.

Many well-known and highly successful books started out with titles that were later changed. According to Dan Poynter, the father of self-publishing:

- *Tomorrow is Another Day* became *Gone With The Wind*.
- *Blossom and the Flower* became *Peyton Place*.
- *The Rainbow Book* became *Free Stuff for Kids*.
- *The Squash Book* became *Zucchini Book*.

- *John Thomas and Lady Jane* became *Lady Chatterley's Lover.*
- *Trimalchio in West Egg* became *The Great Gatsby.*
- *Something That Happened* became *Of Mice and Men.*
- *Catch-18* became *Catch-22.*

An important exercise is to go to a large bookstore. While there, notice how other book browsers go up and down the aisles looking at the shelves. At this point, all they see are book spines and a bit of color and font selection, yet some catch their eye and offer an invitation to be pulled off the shelf. When bookstores present books displayed on tables, it is common to see the browser pick up a book, scan the front and back cover, then put it down again before going on to another. The entire process takes only a few seconds for each book. That is all the time you have to make an impression on a potential reader. In those few seconds, you must appeal to three of the five human senses: sight, speech, and hearing, and figuratively the last two, touch and smell.

> **Sight:** This occurs when potential buyers first come in contact with your book's title and cover. They usually get a glimpse of the name of your book, the spine, the font, and the color scheme. So your title must be presented in an aesthetically appealing manner.

> **Speech:** As browsers' eyes scan your book title, it is highly likely they can hear themselves speak your title in their heads. If they get tongue-tied or stumble over the words, it will add to the difficulty of marketing your book.

> **Sound:** Business philosopher Jim Rohn says that in order to have effective communication, you must "have something good to say, say it well, and say it often." Your title will be heard often, but will it be good and will it be said well?

Touch: Touch also means to "relate to" or "to have an influence on." Figuratively, your title must allow itself to touch or be touched by being able to relate to your readers or have some type of influence on them.

Smell: Your title should figuratively give off an aroma and project "a distinctive quality or atmosphere." If the aroma of the title suggests that very little thought or concern was given, people will assume that the rest of the book is the same way. The title of your book must be powerful in conveying its core message.

The *Publisher's Weekly* bestseller list recently had the following breakdown of book titles. Out of 20 books:

Length	# of Titles
One-word title	1
Two-word title	5
Three-word title	4
Four-word title	5
Five-word title	3
Six-word title	0
Seven-word title	1
Eight-word title	1

The point is that most honchos at major publishing companies believe that the simpler or shorter the title, the better. None of the titles were complex.

Many nonfiction books with short titles have a longer, smaller-print subtitle explaining and reinforcing the title. Here is a classic example of a short title with a subtitle, forming a best seller in the self-help arena: *Crush It: Why NOW is the Time to Cash In On Your Passion*, written by Gary Vaynerchuk. This is an excellent book on branding, and I highly recommend it for your "to read" list. If all of the shortest and best titles are taken, you will need to go on to a bit longer title, but keep it in the theme of answering the primary question.

Consider something like *Social Media: Everything You Ever Wanted To Know But You Couldn't Find The Answer For.* The name should sound good when said aloud. It should be easy to pronounce, and the words should sit well together.

Creating a title that has meaning just for you, as awesome as you believe it to be, is like walking in on the punch line of a joke. You have to be there through the entire joke to get it. Most readers will not get it. So restrain yourself, discipline yourself, and make yourself stick to this important rule.

When looking at titles, also consider checking the statistics of what sells, what moves, and what captures people's attention. In other words, is your subject matter currently relevant or "viral?" If so, even better. Remember the bestselling titles are short, sweet, to the point, and answer a question.

MISSION: THE OUTLINE, AKA TABLE OF CONTENTS

The easiest way to write a book is to use the table of contents as an outline. People get stuck when they think in terms of writing a book. Do not let this delay you. There is a lot of book outlining software available today, but I personally believe they have the potential to cause more distraction then assistance.

The best possible outlines have come from pure "flow." I advise my clients to do a simple process of setting the timer for two minutes and just writing. I ask that they write everything that pops into their heads without thought or judgment on the subject. The questions I ask are: What is most important to you? What do you know a lot about? Tell me 12 things that fall under that subject that are valuable to know. Under each of the 12 things, give me 3 things that are a "must" in that category. Using index cards to write your answers on is a useful way to arrange chapters and sections of your book.

Believe it or not, my students have come up with a table of contents/outline in less than 10 minutes using this method. Our greatest block is that we tend to over think things. We overanalyze, and what happens is that we get into analysis paralysis. Our creativity and "flow" freeze up, and all spontaneity and creativity just exits out of the thought process. When we stall the creative flow by trying to be correct, proper, and appropriate, we end up talking ourselves out of what we intuitively know that we know and into a space of doubt, or what we think we do not know. (You may have to read that twice, but I bet you know exactly what I mean!) You need to be natural, sensible, and reliable, and trust what naturally comes from within you. It works every time.

Let's revisit the social media and question/answer formula from above. The question: Are you overwhelmed with social media? This answer: *Social Media Explained*, right? Simple enough.

It is likely that chapter one would be a brief statement defining what social media is. Chapter two could possibly be a list of social media platforms such as Facebook, Twitter, Pinterest, Google+, LinkedIn, etc. Depending on the scope of your explanation, you could create as many chapters as you want, then add subcategories under each chapter. Some examples of this could be: "Setting Up Your Profile," "Learning the Interface," "Linking To Your Website," etc. Later we will go into how to piece down the portions of the book in more detail.

What I want you to do after this process is to write these outlines on your index cards and then add one or two short sentences to trigger your thought process and match each outline in each heading.

Social Media Explained

Chapter One: Social Media
The History (Who)
How It Works (What)
Channel Overview (Where)
The New Business Tool (Why)

Chapter Two: Setting Up Your Profiles
Facebook
    The History (Who)
    How It Works (What)
    Learning The Interface (How)
    Channel Overview (Where)
    Social Relationships (Why)

Twitter
  The History (Who)
  How It Works (What)
  Learning The Interface (How)
  Channel Overview (Where)
  142 Characters or Less (Why)

Pinterest
  The History (Who)
  How It Works (What)
  Learning The Interface (How)
  Channel Overview (Where)
  A Picture Says It All (Why)

YouTube
  The History (Who)
  How It Works (What)
  Learning The Interface (How)
  Channel Overview (Where)
  Connecting Via Video (Why)

Chapter Three: Getting Social
You Are Ready (Who)
What To Do: Action Steps (What)
Linking To Your Website (How)
Connecting Your Profiles (Where)
Expand Your Reach (Why)

The idea is to keep it very basic and simple at this stage. Write it in outline form on your index cards, and then add a sentence or a short paragraph, which will remind you what the chapter is about. Do not spend too much time trying to organize this. Remember, these are just index cards; you can move them all around, take some away, or add new ones. What works best for me is to lay them on the floor and just keep moving them around like puzzle pieces until I get what looks and feels like the best fit.

Sound easy? It is.

Congratulations! You know how to create an outline and table of contents for your book. Now on to the next mission.

MISSION: COVER DESIGN

When your outline is complete, you can start thinking about the cover and the layout of the inside design. Think of images. Simple is better. Take a good look at books that visually appeal to you and see what it is about them that captured your interest. Make scans or copies of the covers you like, noting the highlighted feature, i.e., I like this font, I like this graphic, I like this color combination, etc. Later, when creating your mock-up or giving direction to your book designer, you will have the samples ready.

Because creative impulse and first instincts are always very valuable, as soon as you have a solid working outline gather your sketches, scans, and notes together for cover and layout design. Collect your ideas in your file folder for Level One.

To properly format the cover of the book you will need a quality image or graphic with a minimum of 300 dpi (dots per inch). Research and locate the best image you can find. This means the image with the highest resolution. If you do not wish to use your own images, you may use royalty-free photographs, which you can find by searching "royalty-free photos" on the Internet.

There are numerous photography sites, such as BigStockPhoto. com, Shutterstock.com, and iStockphoto.com, that offer an array of images for purchase at a nominal fee. Of course, those are the most popular companies. You may also decide to search Google for "royalty-free images," which will link you to numerous other sites. The benefit of the lesser-known sites is that they offer images less seen and used. I have been very lucky with sites that only highlight a handful of photographers and graphic artists.

Once at the site, you may do a keyword search for the type of image you believe would best represent your book cover. Remember to focus on the human senses and to ask questions. Why do you like this image? What draws you to it? Each royalty-free site has different rules, terms, and conditions, so make sure to read the small print and check that you are able to use the image you choose for publication.

The images these sites offer come in several different sizes, so I recommend you select the best-quality file (i.e., highest resolution). This is not an area you want to skimp on; remember, the cover is the first thing your potential customer sees.

Using a professional photograph or graphic is a great investment; after all, we've all come to know that, for better or worse, most books are judged by their covers. Average pricing on many of these sites is offered in credits; small files are normally one or two credits, and the larger files are up to six credits. Pricing is based on how many credits you purchase; a small image is normally $3, where the largest images normally run anywhere between $6 and $18 on average.

You will also want to start thinking about colors and fonts (text types) that you like and may want to use. But do not get too attached to any specific typeset, color, or image. As your book comes together, the "look and feel" you experience when imagining the book will also change based on numerous levels of completion. Use your first instinct to collect some ideas, but then set them aside while you finish the book.

As you study and strategize the bigger picture of what this book means to your brand, your choices may change. Remember that you will be using this book as a business card, so branding and positioning in the correct alignment may need to be expressed in a more powerful way on the cover. It must be simple, effective, and to the point.

You will be giving the book to people and saying, "That's right, I wrote the book on the subject. Here are some answers. Here's my gift to you." And they will be happy to receive offerings from "the expert."

Your book is going to open doors to new opportunities and for getting new and better-quality clients. It works! I know this because I have done it, for myself, for friends, and for clients.

LEVEL ONE RECAP

◉ MISSION: The Title

Why
Questions and Answers
Sound It Out
The Five Senses
Word Count

◉ MISSION: The Outline, aka Table of Contents

Access Flow
Index Cards
Bullet Points
Organizing Layout

◉ MISSION: Cover Design

Color, Font, Typography

MISSION BONUS: Cover Creation Training

I have created a training video just for you where I share my secret strategy for book cover design mock-ups that help me to communicate visually with potential cover artists. This training video is normally only shared with my students, but to assist you today, I invite you to visit the following page to view this video:

www.BeMoreThanYouAre.com/coverpower

Congratulations! You have completed all the requirements to move on to the next level. Set your files aside for the time being and do something awesome to reward yourself. You deserve it!

LEVEL TWO

MISSION: BACK COVER

In the last section, we briefly discussed the cover of your book from a visual standpoint. In this section we will go more in depth about the other elements that make a good book cover.

When you look at any kind of a book, there are certain elements inside that most people don't really consider or even think about when they're reading. However, these elements are seen by our sub-conscious minds and affect our thoughts and opinions about the book. Take the time to familiarize yourself with these elements. As you progress through the writing of your book, consider how to best convey your message, both front and back. After all, a book cover consists of a lot more than just a title.

When someone picks up a book and looks at the front cover for more than a few seconds, then it is highly likely that person will then turn the book over to find out more about the content and the author. When you are thinking about the design for the back of your book, keep in mind that you will need to leave room for the ISBN box and, if you choose, a photograph of you, the author. You also need to decide what type of content you wish to share on the back cover.

Do you wish to share the why, or the reason you wrote the book? Do you wish to ask the question and then explain how this book will answer it? Perhaps you will have some quotes from other experts sharing the benefits they gained from your work. The goal of your book's back cover is strategic placement of sales copy that will sell it to the person reading it. In other words, the text must be so powerful and compelling that it will convince prospective buyers that it is worth their while to invest some cold hard cash and actually purchase the book.

Now that you have ideas for the color, fonts, and images for your book cover, it is time to add them to your file folder. Create a new folder for back cover ideas and look for samples of authors' photos, typesets, colors, graphics, etc. When you have everything gathered for your cover ideas, lay out your clippings and sketches on the table and move them around to see how the pieces fit. Make notes throughout the process. Do the colors clash? Do they offer a nice contrast? Remember that most book buyers purchase online, and that means they are seeing a two-inch representation of your book cover. If you cannot read it at that size, you need to eliminate. Leave space for your ISBN box, which is usually located at the bottom of the book.

I have had several students share that a useful process for them is to "mind map" or "vision board" their book. They include the noteworthy *New York Times* bestseller seal on the front, powerful endorsements and accolades on the back, and the words "over one million copies sold" gracing the front. If this manifestation technique works for you, then by all means use it!

Susan Daffron, known as "The Book Consultant," recommends placing these eight elements on the back cover of your book:

1. **A Compelling Headline.** As with any headline for an advertisement or in website copy, you want your headline to reach out and grab the reader. The headline needs to explain what your book is about in just one sentence or phrase. Writing headlines is an art unto itself, so spend a lot of time crafting this element.

2. **An Introductory Paragraph.** After the headline, you need an introductory paragraph that builds on the benefits you mention in the headline. Draw readers into what your book is about and again explain why this particular book will solve their problem. Determine what it is about your book that makes it different from any other book on the subject, and summarize it in the opening paragraph.

3. **Bullet Points.** The bullet-point list explains the benefits the reader will receive by reading the book. A great bullet point makes the reader want more information. The goal is to intrigue readers so that they are compelled to learn more by purchasing the book.

4. **Testimonials or Endorsements.** These may come from reviewers or peers in the industry. Send out advance review copies to people and ask for endorsements. If you get a fantastic testimonial, it can do double duty as the headline.

5. **An Author Biography.** Explain in a short paragraph why you have the expertise and credentials to write this book.

6. **The Book Category.** Most books include cataloging information on the back cover at the top. This information comes from the BISAC subject headings, which you can find online at the following address:

www.bisg.org/standards/bisac_subject/index.html

7. **The ISBN and Barcode.** The barcode includes the ISBN so that the book can be scanned. In some cases, you may also include the price. Some people opt not to put in a price so they can test different price levels and eventually find the optimum pricing for the book.

8. **A Call to Action.** At the end of your marketing copy, you should include one final "push" to purchase the book.

Now you have a greater understanding of what takes place on the back cover of the book. Go to your library or local bookstore to do some research on this. You will discover that most books incorporate a strong combination of these elements. Your book should too!

MISSION: INTERIOR LAYOUT

Now, on the inside of the book, we have to consider the page layout. Some book interiors are very simple and plain. They have page numbers on the bottom, the name of the book on the top corner of one page, and the name of the chapter on the top corner of the opposite page. Others have fancy design elements that get creative with font, graphic insertion, and formatting. Consider how you are positioning and branding yourself and whether your decisions match your personal brand, the title, and the overall concept of the book.

When formatting, be sure to number the pages correctly. If you look at any book published by a standard publisher, you will see that every book has the odd-numbered pages on the right and the even-numbered pages on the left. If you think about it, when you open the book, the first page you see is page one, and so right-hand pages always have to be odd-numbered pages.

In my book *Reiki for Children*, I chose to do something different. Because it is a book aimed at older children, I wanted the interior to be more visually engaging. I instructed my designer that I wanted the chapter covers to have a different look both in style and size. I also chose to have my pages fit all the way into the corners. On one side is the name of the book, and on the other side, instead of the chapter title, I have the author's name.

There are several questions you should ask yourself in terms of the page layout:

- What's going to be on top?
- What's going to be on the sides or in the margin?
- Do you want a narrow-looking book?
- Do you want it to be spread all the way to the ends?

- Do you want the edge of it to be justified (i.e., to run straight along both the left and right column borders)?
- What's going to be on the bottom? Is it going to be your name? The book name? Can it be a website?

I want you to consider the design of the inside page layout and possibly scan or photograph an idea or layout that you may like for the person who will be laying it out for you. Remember to include this in your file folder for Level Two.

Another consideration is typesetting. I personally like a book with justified text. To justify your text means making the right edge of the type column straight, just like the left edge is. Some people set books with the right side of the column ragged because the lines aren't adjusted to be the same length. This is a publishing no-no and should be avoided. Doing that creates an unprofessional look for a book, and if you research the subject, you will learn that it should not be done.

The front matter of your book (the title pages and everything prior to page 1) should be in lower-case Roman numbers (i, ii, iii, and so on). Reserve using Arabic numerals (1, 2, 3, and so on) for the actual body of the book. A common rule is that page 1 should begin on the first page of chapter one or the introduction. Blank pages should never be numbered. In the body of text or when constructing paragraphs, it is preferable to use either indents or line breaks, but not both.

MISSION: INFORMATION PAGE

When you open any book, the first page you will see is the information page. The information page tells the reader the title of the book and displays the copyright information. If you include art, graphics, illustrations, charts, or photographs within the book, you will add their copyright information as well. It is customary to credit anyone who has assisted with what is displayed within the book, including your book layout or cover designers.

You will also want to include information pertaining to copyright restrictions you have on your work, prohibiting people from taking your work and copying it, making it into a screenplay, distributing in electronic form, etc. Below are some examples:

Example One:
All rights reserved. No part of this book may be reproduced or transmitted in any form or by any means whatsoever without express written permission from the author, except in the case of brief quotations embodied in critical articles and reviews. Please refer all pertinent questions to the publisher.

Example Two:
All rights reserved. No part of this book may be reproduced or transmitted in any form or by any means, electronic or mechanical, including photocopying, recording, or by an information storage and retrieval system—except by a reviewer who may quote brief passages in a review to be printed in a magazine or newspaper—without permission in writing from the publisher.

Additionally, if your book offers any type of advice, you will need a disclaimer. Below are some examples:

Example One:

Although the author and publisher have made every effort to ensure that the information in this book was correct at press time, the author and publisher do not assume and hereby disclaim any liability to any party for any loss, damage, or disruption caused by errors or omissions, whether such errors or omissions result from negligence, accident, or any other cause. Results will vary by reader, and there is direct correlation to effort and time expended.

Depending on if you're writing about health, nutrition, diet, or homeopathic medicine, here is a good example of a disclaimer for that field:

Example Two:

This book is intended as an informational guide. The remedies, approaches, and techniques described herein are meant to supplement not to substitute for professional medical care or treatment. They should not be used for a serious ailment without prior consultation with a qualified health care practitioner.

You are also going to need the include your ISBN number, which you will get later in the process. Make sure to leave room for that number because this is the place where it appears within the book.

You will include a brief summary. By brief, I mean one sentence.

In my book *Reiki for Children*, the summary reads "a manual introducing the healing art of Reiki to children." Normally beneath that you place some category-related keywords. In my case I have "healing," "spiritual exercises," "alternative therapies," "children," "spirituality," "Reiki," "mind and body," etc. Write some ideas into your Level Two file folder but for now keep the space open for these. As you write your book and research further, they may change.

The relevance of what you choose in this space is great because this is how booksellers catalog your book online and off. It tells them where your book should be placed on the shelves in the stores. So again, until you do further research, save the ideas you have, leaving room for super stealth categorizing edits in the near future.

Enter your publisher information. Space permitting, you may also want to put your website address on this page. *Reiki for Children* is actually part of a series called *Family Healing Series*, so I included that information.

I recommend you do some recon on this mission and look at books you have at home. Look at what other books have included to see if it applies to your book as well. Keep in mind that you are the one who creates the text for this page; it does not happen automatically, so gather your research and write. When is the best time to write this content? Now! Complete this mission by the end of the day so you can move on to the next mission.

MISSION: PRE-PAGES

Dedication

The dedication page mentions people whom the author wishes to dedicate the book to. You may want to include who inspired you or the audience you wish to inspire. You may dedicate it to a loved one or someone who motivated you to write the book. The dedication is customarily a personal sentence or two where the author shares a glimpse into his or her personal life. A well written dedication is not only good practice, it aids in positioning you and identifying you with your brand. It has the potential to deepen the reader's connection with you. My advice is to write purely from the heart when you write your dedication.

Preface

The preface is your chance to speak directly to your readers about why you wrote the book, what it's about, and why it's important. You do not need a preface, but it does answer specific questions for your readers. Because it is specifically an introduction to a book, your preface should include information about the book.

Consider including a few or all of the following ideas:

Discuss how the book came about. Why did you choose the particular subject? Why did you write it? Why were you motivated to act on this? How were you inspired? Describe your process and journey of writing the book. Share what you learned, how you felt, and any insights into real-life situations gained through the writing. You may also want to include how you've changed as a person during the process.

Discuss any problems that came up during the journey and how you dealt with these trials and tribulations. Give a brief description of the book, but don't give anything away (after all, they are reading the whole book for that!) State the purpose of the book, especially if the work is nonfiction. For example, if your book is intended to educate the reader about famous CEOs in the 20th century, you may want to state this in the preface. You could also describe what the reader can hope to learn by reading the book.

Share how long it took you to write the book, if it's relevant. For example, if you've been researching Steve Jobs and writing the book for 10 years, you may want to mention this fact to give the reader an idea of the thought and effort you put into the project. If it's a nonfiction book, discuss your research process.

Tell your readers about your sources. Why are they unique? Why is this particular biography of Steve Jobs, for example, special compared to others? If you have a special structure within the book, let the reader know and include any helpful suggestions for following the structure. Finally, remember to keep it short. Two pages are sufficient for a preface.

Foreword

Wikipedia best describes a foreword: "A foreword is a (usually short) piece of writing sometimes placed at the beginning of a book or other piece of literature. Typically written by someone other than the primary author of the work, it often tells of some interaction between the writer of the foreword and the book's primary author, or the story the book tells. Later editions of a book sometimes have a new foreword prepended (appearing before an older foreword, if there was one), which might explain in what respects that edition differs from previous ones."

The Chicago Manual of Style tells us, "The foreword is usually written by someone other than the author or editor, usually someone eminent (to lend credibility to the book), and although the title page may say 'Foreword by X,' if the foreword is only one or two pages (which is normal), the name of the foreword writer normally appears at the end of the foreword. (The title or affiliation of the author of the foreword may also appear there.)."

Many people confuse the foreword with the preface. A good way to remember is that the preface is always written by the author of the book and generally covers the story of how the book came into being or how the idea for the book was developed, whereas the foreword is always written by someone else and often times it is used to lend credibility.

Acknowledgments

It is very important to thank the people who were instrumental in the writing of your book. Depending on the level of formality, these could range from colleagues to editors to family members. Whom do you wish to thank? Who helped you on this journey? Remember to acknowledge those who helped make the book a reality for you.

Author or Editor Bio

The author or editor information or biography often appear at the very back of the book, or, if printed in hard cover, on the back cover flap. Practice your copywriting skills and summarize all of your greatness in one page. Include your personal mission statement or any credibility-lending accolades you have gained on your journey. Your bio in the book is also a branding and positioning resource, so make sure what you write here is in complete alignment and consistent to your brand.

Additional Pages

Finally, we need to consider what comes after the book's body or main pages. In the back matter of the book, you may have appendices, a glossary, references, recommended reading, sources, a bibliography, a reference list, a list of contributors, an index, errata, a colophon, or optional information (bibliographical notes about design, the designer, typography, or other general info about book production, such as "this was a special printing," etc.).

Oddly enough, many people are not aware that when writing your book you must consider all of the above pages. Your mission at Level Two is to write these pages. If you plan on using a foreword, make a list of candidates you would like to contact. If you will be utilizing a ghostwriter or will be inserting private label rights content into your book, exclude them from the above, as I highly recommend you write these pages yourself. They must convey the "voice" of you, the author.

MISSION: THE FRAMEWORK

The main body of your book may contain any of the following: introduction, epigraph, chapter text, afterword, or conclusion. I refer to this as the framework of your book.

Students have told me that their introductions and conclusions were the most difficult parts of their book to write. This is because the introduction and conclusion create a framework of your thoughts around the main body (interior) of the book.

With that imagery in mind, think of the introduction as the hostess at the front door who invites the reader in. She moves them from their own lives into your world, your interior, and she does so in such a way that they feel welcomed and comfortable. This helps the reader to enter your home (your book's interior).

The conclusion is written in much the same way, in the form of a nice hostess who is helpful in transitioning your visitors (readers) back out and into their own lives. This helps them see with more clarity what they learned while in your space and why it should matter to them in reference to their own lives.

Introduction

You never get a second chance to make a first impression. This is where you get your chance to impress! A powerfully written introduction sets the stage for your reader. This is where you focus on language that makes your unique proposition appealing, intriguing, and magnetic. If you are writing nonfiction, it is where you reveal what the entire book is about. It is not formulated or summarized but rather written in a way you would address sales copy. Consider it the preview, trailer, or coming attraction segment of your book.

Create an effective "hook" the way they do in film. You want to capture and captivate your reader in a way that encourages them to read all the way through. In your introduction you offer a promise, and the main body of your book is where you deliver on that promise. Present it in a way that every reader will want to dig in and read right away because of the quality and value of your information.

Conclusion

After you write your conclusion, edit it to make sure you use keywords or parallel concepts and images that you also used in the introduction. Return to the concepts or themes stated in the introduction. This strategy brings the entire journey of your book full circle and wraps up the concept in a way that will impact the reader long after the book has been put away.

When writing your conclusion, avoid writing your beginning with an unnecessary, overused phrase such as "in conclusion," or "in closing." You want to write your conclusion in a way that will push beyond the boundaries, stretch the imagination, and challenge your reader to do the same. Your conclusion must give your readers something to take away that will impact their life in a powerful way. Think of your conclusion as your wish and gift to your readers. Make it exciting and charged in a way that will motivate your readers to take action on what they have learned.

Call To Action

Propose a call to action, a specific course of action, a solution to a problem, a challenge; or offer questions for further study. You want what you have shared to make an impact on your reader and redirect their thought process in a way which helps them to apply your information and ideas to their own lives.

- **MISSION: Back Cover**

  Placement
  Author Photo
  The Eight Elements

- **MISSION: Book Interior Layout**

  Page Style
  Formatting
  Correct Numbering
  Page Layout
  Typesetting

- **MISSION: Information Page**

  Credits
  Copyright
  Disclaimer
  ISBN
  Summary
  Category
  Publisher

- **MISSION: Pre-Book Pages**

  Dedication
  Preface
  Foreword
  Acknowledgments
  Author or Editor Bio
  Additional Pages
  Add-Ons

- **MISSION: The Framework**

  Introduction
  Conclusion
  Call to Action

MISSION PERK: Rest and Recharge

At the completion of this mission, take a break. Step away from your work for a day or two and allow your mind to rest. You have accomplished a lot, and you are nearing completion. I know you may be thinking, "I have not written the book yet," but trust me, the hardest part has passed. After your break and before you move on to the next mission, go back to your Level One file folder and refine your outline. Level Two has provided you with more clarity, and you may be inclined to make some changes at this point. Make them.

MISSION BONUS: Strategy

Refine your outline by asking questions. What I mean by this is to ask the questions your reader would be asking and then answer them in simple sentences. This process may add chapters or subchapters to your book and may be things that you missed the first time around. This "ask the questions" exercise helps you focus on what your reader still needs to know. Remember that, as the expert, you provide your clients with answers, sharing things you have learned through your experience. Offer the same to your readers. Don't hold back, and answer the most pressing and challenging questions you have been asked. Do not concern yourself with formatting at this point; just write sentences or short paragraphs that provide the answers. You will add to this and build upon it in a later level and mission.

Think of this process as piecing together a puzzle. At this juncture you are creating the edges of the puzzle. Do not invite confusion or frustration by attempting to make sense of the random pieces in the middle just yet; instead focus on getting all of your edge pieces lined up, and trust that it will all come together by the end. This exercise is one which I recommend you do again after each day's mission.

This is your draft copy and is meant to be fluid and movable. You can rearrange and expand or reduce. As it comes together you will begin to see patterns and have an intuitive sense of what needs to be included and what needs to be removed. There are no rules that lock anything in place. Depending on the subject of your book and its purpose, you may get as detailed or as deep into each subject as you wish, or create a lot of possibility where readers can construct their own conclusions. The choice is yours. Remember, nothing is written in stone, yet . . . You may cut and paste and move around as you're building. Allow what is inside of you to flow out of and through you. Creativity is the key to this process.

LEVEL THREE

MISSION: TALK RECORDING

What has happened with self-publishing is that the playing field has finally been leveled. Readers communicate differently than they did even five years ago. Today's styles are more relaxed, and we like to read as if we are listening to the author. If you pick up a book from the '40s or '50s, you will instantly recognize a noticeable difference. The books then were very authoritarian. Styles have relaxed substantially since then. This trend makes it even easier to write because today's authors often speak their books into being.

With this method you are able to capture the flow and essence of what is being conveyed easily and quickly. You can bypass writing entirely and "talk" your book into being. This is especially useful for those who have been using the excuse "I'm not a writer."

Imagine the valuable content you will collect if, for example, you have a 45-minute drive to work each day. That's one and a half hours each day where you can press "record" and "write" your book. At the end of the week, you have dedicated seven and a half hours to your book. Have your recordings transcribed and then look at them. I am sure there will be the beginning of a wonderful manuscript in your hands.

Does that sound too good to be true? It is a well-guarded secret, but many authors use this method. The outdated image of sitting over a dusty typewriter staring at blank pages for years is a fallacy and probably designed to keep you from living up to your fullest potential. In the next chapter I share a very powerful story to emphasize this point.

It is my personal belief that each and every person has an obligation to write a book and share, via a unique voice, the way they experience the world as seen through their eyes.

Now imagine that your story—something you have already done, lived, and feel comfortable with—actually has the possibility to bring you the elusive wealth you have been chasing. It is your legacy, and you owe it to the world.

MISSION: BOOK INTERIOR

Here we are, at the actual start of writing the bulk of your book. If you have completed the above two levels, you are excited and super charged to get to it. The first two levels have provided a strong enough argument and roadmap for your book, and I bet you are feeling up to the task of writing, especially since you now have something tangible to look at which represents the scope of what you know.

For those of you super ninjas who love to play, leveling up is fun and easy: just keep racking up the points (in this case the points you present in your book). In my experience, at this level, everything just flows, and many people cannot type fast enough to keep up with their thoughts. Again, I suggest using your secret weapon: a recording device.

Locate something that will record your voice, and then let it all flow out. Release all of your knowledge, experience, and expertise. Share all of your wisdom and learning, shortcuts, and tools. Simply record yourself talking, and then have it transcribed. All of my students at this stage come back to me announcing how surprised they are at the wisdom they have. To illustrate this, allow me to share the story I promised you in the last chapter.

I have a friend who has a pizzeria that has been in his family for three generations. He knows pizza inside and out. He is also an Internet marketer, and despite the fact that the restaurant's neighborhood has gone down in foot traffic and is now devalued, despite the economy and all of the financial troubles currently plaguing millions of small business owners, this man is not only prosperous, but he just opened a second location.

He keeps telling me that he wants to supplement his income online and make money on the Internet. I advised him to write a book. I suggested a book entitled *Marketing For Your Pizza Restaurant*. For those of you frowning at this, allow me to offer the following statistics from the Pizza Power Report:

> **Store Counts:** Compared to the previous year's Pizza Power Report (2005), the total number of pizzerias in the United States dropped by 458 units, a 0.7% decrease, to 69,386 total units. According to the National Restaurant Association, there were approximately 900,000 restaurants in the country at the end of 2005, which means pizzerias comprise 7.7% of all U.S. restaurants.

> **Sales:** For the industry as a whole, sales rose just over $309 million (1%), with overall sales for the pizza segment totaling $31.2 billion for 2005. This represents 7.1% of the overall "eating place" restaurant sales in the United States, which was $437 billion, according to the National Restaurant Association.

That is a massive niche, where I am sure owners need assistance in successful marketing to make sure they do not fall into the 0.7% of restaurants closing!

My friend was quick to argue about not being an author, and he told me that running a place and marketing it were two different things. He closed his argument by sharing that he had no idea how or time to write a book. We engaged in a conversation where I began trying to explain how easy it is to actually write the book, but he had his mind made up: he was not an author, period.

Well, lucky for me, my handy-dandy stealthy mission camera was nearby, and unbeknownst to him, I simply turned it on to record. The image was not important; I just wanted to capture the brilliance and knowledge of what he was saying as he shared his marketing strategies. I asked him specifically how he markets and arranges it so that his employees continue to stay on where at competitive restaurants they leave. I asked for specific things he does that may be responsible for some of his success. At this point, he got very excited (passionate is a better word), and information just came out of him at quantum speed. Thankfully, I captured it all. I uploaded the video to YouTube, selected the option to make the video "unlisted" (only viewable by those who have the actual link), and then posted a job on Fiverr.com with instructions to transcribe a 14-minute video.

Within an hour of his leaving I had completed the mission of recording him, uploading the video (for sound) on YouTube, and sent over my $5 to have it transcribed. The very next morning I had a Word document in my hands. My friend came over about a week later, and as he entered the house I told him, "You won't believe it! You know how last week we were discussing the writing of a marketing book for pizzerias? Well, I found this online, and I want you to read it." Sometimes you have to trick people into recognizing their own potential and greatness!

As he began to read it he began shaking his head . . .

"Wow!" he said as he read the document. "This is amazing! This guy really knows his stuff. This is excellent information." Finally he asked, "Who wrote this?"

I answered, "YOU did!"

"Yeah right. When? In my sleep, or in an alternate life?" came his response. "I couldn't write anything this awesome."

"Yes," I said, "you can and you did."

I turned on the computer, placed him in the chair next to me, put the document into his hands, and said, "Now listen and read."

I turned on the video/audio of his own voice, and when I looked over, he was in tears, crying in disbelief that what he thought was brilliance just moments ago had actually come from within him. It all flowed from a place that he was not consciously aware even existed. His place of truth and authenticity, his place of knowledge and wisdom, his experience and life journey, his heart and soul.

I don't have to tell you how powerful that is; It speaks for itself. It is so powerful, in fact, that it is why I am so driven to help others to write their books and let their inner light shine.

Yes, there are many ways to collect content, but in my experience, the best and most authentic content is one which you speak when you are in moments of flow. You can use any recording device. Do not let the lack of understanding technology slow you down. Ask someone how to turn the damn thing on and record yourself. Remember, you are on a mission to complete the levels and win a better life for yourself and your family. You owe it to them to overcome these obstacles and to see your way through, not to create excuses.

Since discovering this powerful strategy, I have held events where I take regular, everyday people and guide them through this process. This is a strategy I initiate with reluctant authors and experts-to-be. More willing participants simply use the Level One and Two processes, and it jump starts their creativity and flow and they record themselves. The power of this strategy comes from when you just talk or write and not think, not at this critical stage. This strategic tool is so ingenious that the great publishing houses that have locked out authors for centuries consider it their secret weapon. I am happy to share this with you because I know you do not need their support, approval, or branding to let your voice be heard.

You are the Brand.
You are the Platform.
You are the Position.
You are the Expert.
You are the Voice.

Recording your book content is also a useful tool for finding your own voice. This is important because it is the style in which your readers will come to relate to you. The style in which you communicate is also an important component of your brand. Always remember that being authentic and original is best. Don't try to be someone you are not.

Dinty Moore, in *Truth of the Matter*, wrote: "An author's voice consists of many things, including word choice, sentence structure and rhythm, metaphor and imagery . . . perhaps humor or irony, and always the personality of the writer."

A good writer maintains a distinct style throughout the book. It is your expression of personality, and my biggest advice is be YOU (after all, that is who you are). Don't try to write in someone else's voice—be true to your own voice. The general tone should be authentic, truthful, friendly, and helpful, especially in nonfiction.

MISSION: CONTENT CURATION

Where else can content come from? You may have a wellspring of content around you and be unaware of how beneficial it could be to your book. Do you have an online community, hold regular meetings, associate with colleagues, or have mastermind or focus groups? If so, I bet there is a lot of valuable content in there waiting to be discovered. Ask those you value and trust for their thoughts on the subject and offer to interview or record them.

Other ways you can collect content:

> **Summaries:** Gather information from different books, websites, or blogs, and then summarize all of the research.

> **Interviews:** Offer an interview, primarily asking questions and having those interviewed provide most of the content with their answers.

> **Memories, Movement, Methods:** Dig deep and recall stories that show how you moved and progressed, which methods you used, etc.

With the exception of summaries, recording the above is better than trying to write it because the answers come naturally from that place of flow. When we try to write our answers we subconsciously pause to think, and when we think we judge. We begin to want to replace words etc., and this interrupts the creative flow. This is what editors do for you after the fact.

MISSION: PRIVATE LABEL RIGHTS

Finally, we can utilize private label rights, or PLR as they are known. If you have not heard of these before, then let me share another powerful secret and strategy used by other authors and experts. Private label rights are a special type of license or "right to use," which you may purchase. Upon purchase you are legally allowed to rewrite, edit, and publish this written content as your own. You are even allowed and encouraged to include your own name as the author.

Yes, you read that right. You may buy content, put your name to it as the author, and then sell it as your own. And before you judge, allow me to share an industry secret: Many authors and experts have used it to leverage their platforms at one time or another. I've discovered that not only does PLR come in handy to fill in gaps in your writing, it is also awesome for setting a foundation to build product lines on and as website or blog fodder.

PLR articles are a relatively inexpensive way to produce what I call "common filler content" for your book. PLR content helps to keep that flow going and acts as filler in between your written work. The best part about PLR is that you can edit, change, rearrange, rewrite, separate, or combine as you wish; in other words, give it your "voice."

The best use of PLR for common filler content is to "fill in" the basic or rudimentary parts that need explanation. For example, if your book is about *My Secret To The Greatest Gardens*, then you will most likely include some chapters on basic things like soils, climates, etc. Your primary contribution to the book is the unique blend of techniques that you have gained through your experience. You do not need to reinvent the wheel in discussing soil and climate basics. This is where some PLR can come in very handy.

If you think about it, this makes sense. Used strategically, PLR has the power to grow your traffic, build your list, and inspire more of your writing (books or products) than you've ever imagined.

Another example demonstrates the best place for inserting some PLR into your book. Let's imagine you are writing about preparing to paint a house. You locate several articles that outline the basic steps to get ready. Again, why reinvent the wheel? How differently can you explain to someone that they need to go to the store and buy paints and brushes? How many unique ways can something like that be expressed? Some types of factual things just need to be stated as a part of your larger explanations or descriptions, and if they have already been written in PLR, why would you want to spend precious time outlining those basics?

Private label rights usually come in the form of articles, and these articles are named in ways that describe what the article is about. At the bottom of each article there is usually a word count, and some also provide useful keywords. Again, should you wish to use any of these in your book, on your blogs or for website content, you are free to do so. However, Google recognizes duplicate content for published works online; therefore I highly recommend that you reserve their use for "filler content," meaning that you use specific combinations of sentences combined with your own writing.

A combination of two or three 400+ word articles could easily be used as a starting point for your own writing, combining it with some of the PLR which can then be repurposed into a hearty chapter for your book. As you read through your PLR articles, have your notepad or Word document ready. Copy and paste any powerful sentences onto the notepad or your Word document. Do not worry if they do not string together in any specific order at this point; you will be able to move them around and string them all together with your own style and voice later.

As you continue reading you'll notice that some content you will decide to bypass, while other parts can be quite powerful. This process is also useful to trigger your own writing to come forth. When you find specific sentences or paragraphs that resonate with your style, you should elaborate and add some of your own words to them. Then you will continue to go on to the next one. Repeat this process until you have gone through all of the PLR articles from your list or until you have finished pulling content out of each specific article.

It pays to really take the time to familiarize yourself with the content and go through several of the different categories. You will notice that quite a few of them have articles with information which will provide powerful content filler for your book.

MISSION: GHOSTWRITER

The final option to have your book completed is to hire a ghostwriter. The challenge with this option is that it is important to note that your voice is an integral part of your branding. When you hire someone else, what your readers will ultimately get is their voice. When they see you later at your website or on your social media, your voice will not be the same. This will trigger a feeling of inconsistency when relationships need to be built upon trust and authenticity. Your audience will eventually come to think you are not the "real deal" and will find another to replace you.

Finally, your book is a springboard and launching pad to greater things, such as speaking, interviews, a product line, etc. Will your ghostwriter be available for all of that as well? How will you be able to "ghostwrite" your way through an interview? Hence the reason I stress speaking in your own voice. You may think you are not perfect, but your authenticity will speak in volumes to your followers, and they will be customers for life if they see your true being.

LEVEL THREE RECAP

- **MISSION: Book Interior**

  Recording Devices
  Free Video: YouTube.com
  Outsource Resource: Fiverr.com
  Finding Voice

- **MISSION: Content Curation**

  Groups, Memberships, Meetings, Masterminds
  Summaries
  Interviews
  Memories, Movement, Methods

- **MISSION: Private Label Rights**

  Basics
  Why Reinvent The Wheel?
  Combining Content
  Building on Sentences

- **MISSION: Ghostwriter**

  Your Voice vs. Their Voice

MISSION PERK: Download PLR Bonus Pack

As a perk for your hard work and efforts thus far, I have decided to give you a gift to help you see what PLR looks and feels like. When you go to the following page, you will be able to download my "Super Filler PLR" pack, which has filler for almost every niche.

www.BeMoreThanYouAre.com/212plrmission

MISSION BONUS: Expansion Strategy

You do not have to limit yourself to any specific category when it comes to using the private label rights articles. Expand your research. Chances are high that various articles could fill other chapters in your book. An example of this would be a book entitled *How To Build An Online Presence*. Do not limit your search to "online presence." Expand your search to incorporate what else fits. "Blogging" is a part of online presence. "Blog marketing" is a part of that. "All about blogs" is a part of it. Articles on marketing, putting articles on the Internet, doing affiliate sites, etc., are all part of "building an online presence." The list can go on and on, and you can keep going and going looking for different articles that would work. Articles about computers and laptops, copyrighting, and creating an online business could also be used in the *How To Build An Online Presence* example that I used above.

Another example of this is for the imaginary author writing a book we'll call *Easy Marketing*. Do you agree that the reader of this book would also find value in information about list building and auto-responders? So I took a look at the list building and auto-responder PLR articles. I also located several "converting visitors into subscribers" articles that would be very powerful for this book about building an online presence in conjunction with marketing with ease. I also discovered an article titled "Using Free Reports to Build Your List." Of course, this information will provide significant contribution relevant to the readers of this book. To me it's like having a staff of very good interns at my fingertips!

LEVEL FOUR

In this mission you will review all of the data you have written and collected thus far. Lay out your data in such a way that you will get inspired and activate that creative flow. What you currently have in your file folders contains the foundation, framing, roof, and floors of your house. Imagine that writing the filler is much like shopping for the interior of this house. You need to add in the cupboards, select the paint, place the fixtures, and install the faucets. When this is complete it is time to go furniture shopping to get all you need for that home theater or spa.

MISSION: MAPPING

Gather all of your notes and what you have written from your file folders. Arrange it in a way that makes sense to you. The goal of this mission is to take your reader from point A with the introduction to point B with the conclusion.

Look at what you have so far. What is missing from your map? Did you leave out a specific step? Is there a shortcut you forgot to mention? Are you remembering that you wanted to add a special key to pass on or access to a secret passageway? Did you want to share an anecdotal illustration from your own journey? Add these notes now and then rearrange again so that your map gets the reader there in the fastest and most efficient way possible. Where can you streamline the route? What is missing?

MISSION: PACKING BY STACKING

Every successful journey needs a map and specific equipment to get there. Have you ever gone camping only to discover that you left something really important for a happy camping experience at home? You never give so much thought to it until you are there and realize how important it is. "Oh, I remember, last year we pulled the tent posts out of the bag when we cleaned the garage." You are probably laughing out loud remembering a similar experience, and though yours may be a bit different ("I am in Hawaii, and I forgot to pack my bathing suit"), the moral remains the same. This mission will help you make sure to pack everything for your launch.

Get your recording device ready.

Now that your outlines, before and after pages, and PLR notes are organized, turn on your recording device and read out loud what you have in front of you. When you come to the end of a powerful sentence, see if there is anything you forgot to add. Speak it all out loud.

See if you can change what you just spoke into a question. If so, what is the answer to that question? Can you elaborate on the answer and stretch it a bit? You may realize you need to add a link, some resources, or a screenshot. Say out loud, "Note to self: Get those screenshots demonstrating how to get from here to there." As you speak you may realize that this is where you want to insert a well-chosen quote, a reference to another expert you may have encountered, or a clip of his or her material. Be sure to give proper credit, and continue this process until you have gone through everything you have collected in your folders thus far.

This is not the time to worry about perfect grammar or the structure of sentences. This process is simply to assist you in mining for all of the diamonds within, all of the good, fresh, and original content, and to show you that it is always ready to come forth as long as it is invited and given an opportunity to show itself. Do this throughout the day in 30-minute increments. Set a timer and force yourself to get up, walk around, get a light snack, stretch a bit, step outside for a few minutes, shoot some hoops, and then get back to it. You'll be surprised how a little fresh air and exercise brings on a wave of new inspiration.

Keep recording, especially that which you may think is insignificant. That is where hidden gems exist. Remember to pose everything as a question and provide the answer. Every now and again ask "why?" and answer that too. Answering the "why" question will keep your thoughts from becoming too vague or scattered. These answers will also provide rich content that will propel the reader forward. Don't just state a fact; tell the reader why that fact is important. Be as detailed as necessary for complete understanding, and over express and deliver rather than leaving out any detail. Remember, you will be able to edit out what you choose not to include, and that is much easier than adding content in after the bulk of your book is written.

MISSION: TRANSCRIBE

Collect all of the recordings from the last mission. If you have not yet gotten any interviews or other earlier recordings transcribed now is the time to transcribe them as well. You may use providers at Fiverr.com for short recordings, but for longer recordings or a set of them, it may be more cost effective to go to an outsource site such as Guru.com or Elance.com. Anything else you will add from this point will be typed into your document.

MISSION ALERT

Do not attempt to transcribe yourself because you will be tempted to rewrite your pure content. Your analytical or thinking mind will take over, and you'll end up writing a completely different book. Trust me on this!

When your transcribed documents are returned, arrange them in the order of your outline. Read it to see what you may have left out, and prepare to be surprised by what awesomeness came forth. If reading anything specific triggers more content to flow forth, insert it now.

Once again, arrange any transcribed interviews and rearrange as necessary to have a nice flow to your book. Are you sure you have added the PLR if you are using any? Have you added the interview segments or resources you wanted to list? As you go through the book, if anything jumps out at you as missing, insert it now.

It may sound a bit tedious, but it is the best way to write your book without getting stuck in a mental block. It's a mission strategy that works! Simply focus on completing the mission at hand before moving on to the next mission.

When you complete this mission, print what you have so far.

LEVEL FOUR RECAP

⊙ MISSION: Mapping

Getting from A to Z
Streamlining the Route

⊙ MISSION: Packing by Stacking

Leave Nothing Behind
Turn It Into Questions
Diamond Mining

⊙ MISSION: Transcribe

Collect All Recordings
Mission Alert
Contact a Professional
Printing

MISSION PERK: Celebrate

Do something special for yourself. Celebrate that you have come this far. You have almost completed your book. How does it feel, holding all of that paper in your hands? Did you think you'd come this far?

Congratulations!

LEVEL FIVE

MISSION: YOUR EDIT

You are now holding your manuscript! In this mission, you will edit for flow and completion and do a final review of the document. As you read through, make sure that the end of each section or chapter flows into the next.

A helpful strategy for this is to ask yourself these questions when thinking about how each chapter or section concludes: Why is this significant? Why should the reader care? As I mention throughout the book, the "why" is vital. The purpose of your nonfiction book is that your readers gain an understanding of the material. Using the strategy of explaining with "why" is helpful in achieving this effectively.

Once again, read through quickly and efficiently—you aren't editing for structure, grammar, etc. just yet. This edit is your final edit for how the material flows. Remember the metaphor of filling your house with the fixtures and decorations? Now that you have filled it with some furniture, moved it all around a bit, added some accessories, curtains, rugs, and toys, and step away for a moment to consider your work as a whole. Admit it: You know it all looks good!

I'll bet you have surprised yourself with how quickly and efficiently you have completed the previous levels and missions.

Do not continue to the next mission until you are completely satisfied with what you have done so far.

MISSION: REPLAY

In this mission, you will now revisit the cover design and interior layout of your book a final time. You have a completed manuscript in your hands, and you are almost ready to go to print. Make sure you have gotten back your final quotes or mock-ups and that the title, cover text, and design are up to your expectation and brand. Have this all ready, but do not order any book covers yet, because you still don't know what size the book will be, how many pages it will have, etc., and all of that information must be provided when designing the book cover.

MISSION: WRAP-UP

In this mission you are satisfied with your previous missions and are excited to get your book into your readers' hands. You will not want to do the final edit. Some people outsource this final edit, and that is fine as long as you instruct the writer to not make any changes, only suggestions. You do not want an overly obsessive stickler for words to cut your voice out of your book! Remember, no human is perfect, and some of the consistent "flaws" in your language may be a big part of your voice and brand.

If you do decide to outsource your edits, make sure the person is a native speaker in your language (in other words, you do not want someone in India or the Philippines editing your American English manuscript). Ideally, you will locate someone in your community who knows you personally and is familiar with the unique way you communicate. This would be your best course.

Remember to PRINT your final work and make sure to read it and re-read it several times to correct any errors. I suggest printing your pages and reading on paper. When reading online you tend to miss mistakes, and if your service provider is charging per revision, you are paying for mistakes that could have been avoided.

I have also asked friends and colleagues to read and add notes or suggestions to my manuscripts because sometimes we get so wrapped up in our own work, we miss the simple yet obvious.

Do not skimp on content. To have a book that looks and feels like a "real book" in your hands you will need content that fills at least 140 pages. Besides, you want to give your reader the best of what you've got. The more, the better, as they will be grateful for your knowledge and will value you more for not holding back.

You may want to copyright your book professionally, and in the past this was done sufficiently enough by mailing yourself a postmarked copy of the manuscript. If you wish to have a professional copyright, you must register with the US Copyright Office. Below is the link to their fact sheet for books:

www.copyright.gov/fls/fl109.html

MISSION ACCOMPLISHED

You wrote a book. And you know it's not only good, it's great. You know that this is the best of the best because it is authentic and true and comes from your heart with the intention of helping those you serve to the best of your ability.

The only remaining question is: How do you get it into the hands of your readers, and fast?!

LEVEL FIVE RECAP

- **MISSION: Your Edit**
  Flow and Completion

- **MISSION: Replay**
  Cover Text and Design

- **MISSION: Wrap-Up**
  Final Edit

The next level may have the most relevance to your chances at best-seller status and making money with your book. It is based on the critical input of information during the process of signing up your book at CreateSpace and Kindle Direct Publishing.

LEVEL SIX

MISSION: ON TARGET

Having a book is not only about writing it, making it available, and then waiting for sales to come in. It takes some strategic thinking and research on your part to work with Amazon in a way that will position your book in front of the most buyers.

Amazon has something called "ranking," and it is how they categorize and present each book. They rank the books in the following order (and yes, the list below is in order of importance):

- Title
- Category
- Search Keywords
- Author
- Description

Title
Your title must be relevant to the keywords you choose. An example of this would be the term "inner child." If the keyword you select is "inner child," then the best possible title for your book would be

Inner Child and then you can add more (i.e., *Inner Child: How to Heal Past Wounds*).

Remember to keep the keyword first. To use our *Inner Child* example again, *How to Heal Past Wounds: Embracing the Inner Child* is a perfect example of how NOT to name your book. Yes, the keyword is in the title, but it is at the end.

The closer your title comes to your keyword, the better, because Amazon ranks and performs very much like Google and other search engines. The same way you would perform SEO (search engine optimization) on your website, you must consider these critical decisions when presenting your book.

Additionally, similar rules apply to Amazon as they do to Google regarding spamming. You do not want to use keyword-packed titles that make no sense. A workshop I attended taught me this principle with the following example: *Weight Loss Secrets: Lose Weight Fast*. That does pack in the keywords, but the meaning is also relevant; in other words, it makes sense to title this particular book in this way. The above is an example of not using it in a spam-like way.

Of course you want to capture the reader's attention, and that is hard to do in a minimal amount of words, but the shortest and most direct route is always the most effective.

Category

At this time, Amazon and Kindle Direct Publishing both allow you to choose two categories. Choose wisely. This is just as important as your title, so do the same research, and adjust your title if necessary. The goal is to find an exact match for both your title and category.

Now I know this means delving into research of all the categories relevant to your subject matter. But trust me on this: This is of the utmost importance. Over the course of time, and even with no further promotion, your book will continue to rank high and bring in those residual royalty checks every month. The category you select should be broken down to the most minuscule category, because your goal is to go to #1 in that category and then climb your way up.

An example of this is my book *Reiki for Children*. The title includes "Reiki," and the category is "Reiki." I do not have to do anything to promote the book, but because of the title and category match, I have steadily generated a residual stream on that book for over 10 years.

Search Keywords
- How will people find your book?
- What phrases will they search for?
- Learn how to use Google's free keyword tool.
- Use keyword phrases with at least 1,000 searches per month.

You are allowed five keywords. Your first keyword should be an exact match to your book title and category. The second should be the exact phrase of your complete title and keyword. The next few should be words very closely related or even synonyms for what your main keyword is. Just like with Google, rankings now like to look at what Google called "long tail keywords." Long tail keywords are defined as keyword phrases that consist of between two and five words, usually used when searching for a rather specific item.

As always, spending time researching search trends is important. While you may match title to category to keyword, if it is an unknown term and people are not using that language or searching for it, your book will be lost and unsuccessful both in sales and in rankings.

Author

As you construct this page, it is important to make your correct brand impression. If you already have a known brand and all of your books will be in the same niche, consider using that in your author section. An example of this would be "relationship guru." However, if you wish to grow your brand and position to add other services and books in slightly different subject areas, this can strongly work against you. Choose wisely, as Amazon/Kindle frowns upon abusing your author position. If you have a co-author or publisher, editor, multi-authors, etc., use the above reasoning when entering their names.

Book Description

Most authors hurry to write this first, as they see it as an opportunity to share more about their book, but as far as rankings go, it is last in the ranking system. However, once the readers are on your page, they like to read the description, and having a good description is invaluable for selling your book.

Write a description that clearly defines the purpose of the book. CreateSpace's description suggestions say, "A good description may be started by completing this sentence: My book _____who want _____ get _____. Then, add your competitive advantage."

The example they give is "My book helps women who want to improve their health get the best information on healthy dieting for a longer, healthier life. Its unique advantage is that it was based on the author's actual life experience."

If you can work your title, category, and keyword into your description, all the better. But remember that less is more in this case. Your readers want to know about your book and not read an entire chapter; if they do, they can do that in the "look inside" feature at Amazon. At the description stage, all they really want to know is if your book addresses their question or need. If your book is more complex, then look at your competitor's books that are ranking #1 bestseller and see how they describe their book.

You can wrap up your description by closing with a one-sentence mission statement. A great way to find focus is to answer your own question of why you wrote the book to begin with. Identify the specific objectives and goals you want your book to achieve. Write it in a "call to action" format so they feel prompted to act now on buying your book.

The description is about sales and not about optimizing the page, so use your language to convey your best "pitch" for your book. This is the purpose of your book description and the secret to writing one that converts shoppers into buyers.

MISSION: STRATEGIC REWRITE

Now that you have been programmed with the stealthy secret information above, I recommend you go back and reconsider, for the final time, the title of your book. You may want to consider reworking some chapter names. Additionally, with this new information, take a fresh look at your author bio and see if it needs any polishing.

Use this information to refine and super-tune any wording or placement that will both align with your brand as well as position you in the best possible way for sales. Completion and understanding of the Level Six mission gives you super powered ninja moves to launch your book with intelligent power. You are advised to re-read this a few times for mastery on the subject before you move on to the next level.

LEVEL SIX RECAP

- **MISSION: On Target**

  Amazon Ranking System
  Title
  Category
  Search Keywords
  Author
  Description

- **MISSION: Strategic Rewrite**

  Re-polish
  Refine

LEVEL SEVEN

MISSION: SPECIAL ACCOUNTS

In this mission I will familiarize you with CreateSpace and Kindle Direct Publishing (KDP). These are the sites I recommend you use to have your book published on Amazon and Kindle. CreateSpace also allows for you to purchase copies of your own book at minimal cost, and there are no book minimum requirements, so you can order 1 copy or 1,000 copies, there is no difference.

This mission requires you to login to CreateSpace and KDP. In the past I would share screenshots with my students as I walked them through, but nowadays Amazon has so streamlined the process that a child could do it. Remember, you are on a mission, and you will not let the technology get in your way.

CreateSpace

www.createspace.com

Go to the website. They have a very user-friendly interface that is simple to access. The site looks like this when you first arrive:

The process is rather self-explanatory; simply follow the prompts. You will need to provide your email address, a password, your first and last name, the country you reside in, and then select "book" when they ask "What type of media are you considering publishing?"

You will get a prompt asking if you wish to be contacted. The choice is entirely yours, but I believe you are ready to go on your own—after all, you've completed the previous five levels and all of the missions within. I do suggest that you go ahead and select "Send me Updates and Promotions" because occasionally they send valuable information for authors concerning changes and updates. When you have filled in all of the information, click "Create My Account."

When you complete that step, you will be taken to "Member Agreement." As they suggest, please read the membership agreement contained on this page and signify you agree to all its terms and conditions using the radio buttons below, then press "Continue" at the bottom. You will then reach a page that asks you to "Please Verify Your Email Address."

You will see a message that says, "Thanks, your CreateSpace member sign-up is almost complete. Just one more step to get you started."

Go to your inbox for the email address you entered at registration. There should be a message from CreateSpace whose subject heading is "CreateSpace–Verify Your Email Address."

There are two ways to verify:

1. Open the email and click the verification link.
2. Open the email, copy the verification code, and then, back at the CreateSpace page, input it into the select box.

The following screenshot shows what your welcome page should look like:

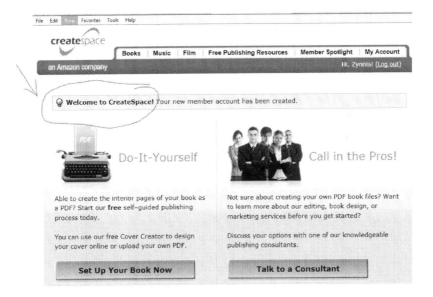

I recommend you select and click "Set Up Your Book Now." When you do you will be taken to the following page:

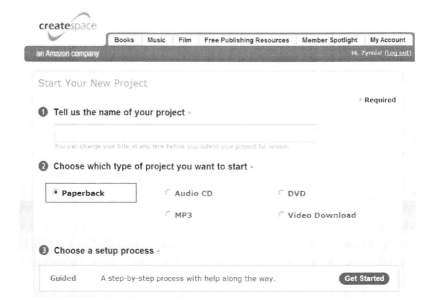

There are three options on this page:

1. Project Name (you may change this at any time)
2. Type of Project: Choose "Paperback"
3. Setup Process: Select "Guided" since this is your first time

The page you are sent to next is where we will input your book information, but that is a later mission. At this time, you are all signed up with CreateSpace and this part of the mission is complete. To return to CreateSpace, simply return to the website once again and login with the user name and password you just entered to sign up. Make sure to store your login information somewhere you will not forget, like the inside cover of your Level One file.

Kindle Direct Publishing (KDP)

www.kdp.amazon.com

Go the website. Amazon's Kindle Direct Publishing (KDP) allows you to self-publish your books and make them available on Kindle, iPad, iPhone, Android, Blackberry, and Mac and PC computers.

Because it is very likely you have used Amazon.com in the past, KDP will prompt you to sign in with your Amazon.com email and password.

You may do this separately, or you can wait to upload your book to CreateSpace, and when your book is live you can select to have it sent to KDP for you. Though they both come through Amazon, CreateSpace has a separate user interface. If you do not have an existing Amazon.com account, sign up by following the prompts in the same fashion as when you signed up for your CreateSpace account. When you get to the page asking for your book information, stop. Go get yourself a beverage and pick up your file folders and manuscript. This is a level you worked hard to attain. Congratulate yourself for getting this far and move on to the next mission.

MISSION: OPERATION SETUP

Making It Real

Sit back down at the computer, take a deep breath, and input the information on the page asking for title, subtitle and the magic word: AUTHOR. The page looks like this:

The rest of this is, again, self-explanatory. Were there any contributing authors? If so, the box will show options in a drop-down format where you may include anyone who assisted you with the writing of your book. Is this a part of a series or a special edition? Select your language and publication date and click "Save & Continue." If there are any errors or information missing, the system will prompt you to make necessary corrections.

ISBN

An ISBN, or International Standard Book Number, is a unique 10- or 13-digit number assigned to every published book. An ISBN identifies a title's edition, publisher, and physical properties such as trim size, page count, and binding type.

With CreateSpace, you have four ISBN options: You can either use a CreateSpace-assigned ISBN, a custom ISBN, a custom universal ISBN, or you can use your own ISBN. Both custom ISBN options are offered through an agreement with Bowker®.

CreateSpace ISBN numbers are fast and inexpensive, and your books get expanded distribution. This offers you the opportunity to access a larger audience through more online retailers, bookstores, libraries, academic institutions, and distributors within the United States.

Before deciding upon a selection, go to CreateSpace.com and type "ISBN" into the search box. They have in-depth information about which option will be best for you.

The next page you arrive at is where you enter or select your ISBN number. During the title setup process, if you use your own ISBN, you will also need to enter your imprint or the name of your publishing company. CreateSpace does verify ownership and authenticity of all ISBNs.

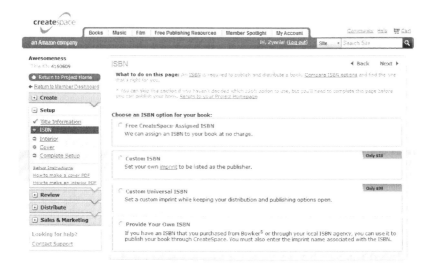

You will have to make a selection before you can proceed.

Each option is briefly explained, and your selection is a personal choice. I have used the CreateSpace ISBN for all of the books I have written thus far. Making a selection here is important because at this juncture, waiting on the ISBN is the only thing that has kept your book from being professionally laid out. You may click on each selection, and a drop-down window will be displayed which gives more detail about each option. Continue with whichever selection you make until your ISBN number is assigned. Once you have your ISBN number, you may move on to the next mission.

MISSION: OPERATION INSIDE JOB

The next section you will be shown is the Interior section. In this section you will be prompted to select trim size, interior type, and paper color.

The menus that you get for your book are going to be based on how your interior is set up. If you really want to have a full-color book, know that book prices are going to be $8 or $9 to print because of the color, leaving you a small profit margin. Therefore, I would suggest selecting black and white, and then I would suggest white for page color. Cream is a little bit more expensive, while white is standard.

Your selected paper color (cream or white) and whether you choose a black and white or full color interior will affect your royalties. Before you decide upon these settings you need to do another bit of recon.

MISSION RECON
CreateSpace has nifty little "What's This?" links in places where people ask the most questions, so if you do not understand something, click on those links. They open a pop-up window the size of an index card that gives you an explanation to help you understand.

I recommend a trim size of 6 × 9 inches, as that is the standard, but they do offer an array of sizes. You will also see that on this page that they offer an option that says "Talk with us about Professional Design Services starting at $249." This is their upsell to book layout services because until your book's interior is properly formatted, you cannot upload the file (well, you can upload a file, but it will look horrible!). You have been patient this whole time—now you need to wait while your book interior is formatted properly.

Why did I wait for this step? Because you needed to complete the prerequisite missions to attain your ISBN. Now that you have it, you may go back into your final manuscript draft and insert it into the space on the information/credits page. You also have the information from Level Six, which will assist you in selecting the best categories for shelving your book. Additionally, you may want to credit the person who does your interior, asking them to input their name as well as the cover designer. (Can you guess your next mission?)

Make sure to tell your book interior designer that you need an exact page count for CreateSpace to order your cover design. Alert them to keep space open for the cover designer's credits as well if you so wish. Request that the page count come to you as quickly as possible so you can mark this mission complete.

MISSION BONUS: Secret Strategy

Make sure that whoever you hire allows you at least one revision. This is because when my layout is complete, I print it and read through the paper copy for a final edit. It is easy to catch any previously missed errors when reviewing the actual paper copy. If you catch any of these errors, you can correct them, send it back to the designer, and then upload your finalized manuscript to CreateSpace.

MISSION: OPERATION COVER-UP

I suggest that you create a proposal asking for a book cover design and upload any print specifics or mock-ups and design ideas you have collected. I highly recommend outsourcing your cover design to a professional who has a well-trained eye for font styles, color combinations, and layout. I have always outsourced my book covers, and a realistic estimate for such work is between $100 and $250.

MISSION PERK: Sample Letter for Outsourcing Cover Design

Project Title
Book Cover for CreateSpace Specs

Project Description
I have written a book, and I need a properly formatted cover to submit to CreateSpace.com.

My cover must be a single (one-piece) PDF that includes the back cover, spine, and front cover.

Below are the requirements for book cover submissions on CreateSpace:

For Black and White–Interior Books:
White paper: multiply page count by 0.002252
Cream paper: multiply page count by 0.0025

For Color-Interior Books:
Multiply page count by 0.002347

More information is at the following link:

www.createspace.com/Products/Book/CoverPDF.jsp

I have attached several mock-ups of how I imagine the cover design to appear; however, I trust your expertise and would appreciate your suggestions and ideas.

I would like the final file to be delivered in 400 dpi and CreateSpace ready.

My budget for this is $150, and I need the project to be completed within one week.

If you research book cover design on Google, you will find that most book cover designers charge between $500 and $3,500.

MISSION: SPINE

The spine width is based on the number of pages in your book. As you can see in the mission perk above, I added the specific requirements for the job. This is very important for your cover to appear properly wrapped around the book. For your information I have included a couple of sample measurements below directly from CreateSpace:

For Black and White–Interior Books:
White paper: multiply page count by 0.002252
Cream paper: multiply page count by 0.0025

Example of spine-width calculation for a 60-page black-and-white book printed on white paper: $60 \times 0.002252 = 0.135$ inch

For Color-Interior Books:
Multiply page count by 0.002347

Example of spine width calculation for a 60-page color book: $60 \times 0.002347 = 0.141$ inch

CreateSpace offers free tools and professional services to assist you during the publishing process. Whether you need a little guidance or help with every detail, their publishing consultants can customize a solution to meet your needs and budget.

They also offer tools such as their Interior Reviewer and Cover Creator. These allow you to do-it-yourself easily and with good results. Cover Creator is the free online tool for designing a professional-quality book cover using your own photos, logos, and texts. I recommend you try to work with it while waiting for your design to come back. If you have any design experience, you may find it an excellent resource to create all of your own future covers. Additionally, you can also select the option to have their team design a professional cover design. Their prices start at $299.

As you can see from above, there are various options available. My advice is to not linger on this mission too long. If you are looking to save money or do it yourself, you may try to create your cover yourself. The way their settings are structured, you can reject or delete any files you are not fully satisfied with, so do not be afraid to play a little bit on the back end.

LEVEL SEVEN RECAP

- **MISSION: Operation Accounts**

  CreateSpace
  Kindle Direct Publishing (KDP)

- **MISSION: Operation Setup**

  CreateSpace Title
  Page Interior
  Hiring the Designer

- **MISSION: Operation Inside Job**

  Final Interior Layout to Specs

- **MISSION: Operation Cover-Up**

  Final Cover Design to Specs

- **MISSION: Spine**

  Specs and Measurement

- **MISSION PERK: Sample Letter for Outsourcing Cover Design**

MISSION RECON

Remember to do some useful recon while waiting for your interior and cover designs to come back. Continue to familiarize yourself with their interface. I recommend you browse their free publishing resources. Watch any tutorial videos, read articles, enter the discussion forums, and engage in the community. It is there for your benefit and further understanding of how these two self-publishing giants work. Use this opportunity to study all of the tools they make available to their authors.

LEVEL EIGHT

MISSION: FILE UPLOAD

When your interior and cover designs come back and you are satisfied, it is time to sign in to www.CreateSpace.com. On the left navigation panel you will select "Interior." You will need the final PDF from your designer as well as the bleed information (ask your designer for this specific).

After you upload your interior file you will want to select "Cover" in the left navigation pane (appears right under/after Interior) and repeat the process with uploading your PDF print-ready cover. Your cover must be a single PDF that includes the back cover, spine, and front cover as one image. You can submit your cover on any size page as long as the printable area is:

- Measured exactly to your book's trim size, spine width, and 0.125-inch bleed
- Centered horizontally and vertically

If formatted correctly, you will be able to see a virtual copy of your book. CreateSpace has a new tool that will show you how your book will look at final print. If anything is not correct (spine, interior formatting, etc.) the tool will alert you, and you will have to correct the errors by notifying your designers. For example, let's say that the photographs on the interior pages will not print well. This tool will tell you that you need to upload a larger file with higher resolution and dpi.

When your design is accepted as formatted correctly, you will have the option to accept and complete setup. You will receive an email from CreateSpace within 24 hours with the next steps to take. While they review your book, you will not be able to upload revised .PDF files or edit your book's information.

After you receive the approval email, you will be able to order your review copy. The review process will commence when you approve the proof copy.

You did it!

Mission accomplished.

Your sample copy is on its way, and in a few short days you will have *your* book in your hands.

Celebrate!

MISSION: DISTRIBUTION

While you wait for your review copy in the mail, you should set up your distribution channels. Before you can enter this information, a pop-up window will appear prompting you to add royalty payment information.

Royalty payment profile. It has a nice ring to it, doesn't it? Click the "Complete your royalty payment profile" link, and you will be asked to enter your Social Security or Tax Identification Number as well as the information for the bank where you want your royalty payments deposited.

Channels

After you enter your royalty information, return to the navigation pane and select "Channels." You will be shown the following options.

> **Standard Distribution** includes your book appearing in the following channels:
>
> Amazon.com
> Amazon Europe
> CreateSpace e-Store

Expanded Distribution is a paid upgrade for your book, which adds:

Bookstores and Online Retailers
Libraries and Academic Institutions
CreateSpace Direct

Each channel has a clickable "What's this?" where, once again, if you click, a pop-up window will display with greater detail. CreateSpace has made this very simple and provides useful and practical tools. I encourage you to explore them.

I also strongly recommend upgrading to Expanded Distribution. Not only will it expand the visibility of your book, your royalty payments are much larger when you sell directly from your store.

That's right, CreateSpace will even give you your own special website link to your e-store where you can sell your books in bulk, offer discount codes, etc.

Pricing

When deciding how much your book will cost, you will want to see how much money will be made from the sales of your book. CreateSpace has an easy tool to help you calculate.

Visit the following page:

www.createspace.com/Products/Book/

When pricing your book:

- Check out the competition.
- Price lower to sell more volume.
- Price higher if you have an original idea for eager readers.

You can see that CreateSpace has tabs that run horizontally across the page: Overview, Cover, Interior, Printing Options, Distribution, Royalties, and Buying Copies.

I recommend you read each one of these tabs.

Royalty Payments

To calculate how much you will be paid in royalties, simply select "Royalties." Once again, you will want to study the information on the page to gain a deeper understanding. In this case they provide a video, and I suggest you watch it. CreateSpace says, "You earn royalties every time we print a book to fulfill a new customer order placed on Amazon.com, Amazon's European websites, your CreateSpace e-Store, or through sales channels offered with Expanded Distribution."

Scroll to the bottom of the page, where you will see the calculator. You will need to know the trim size, number of pages, and interior type. Based on that and your selling price, the calculator will show you how much you will collect in royalties.

Buying Copies for Yourself

Buying copies for yourself is referred to as "Member Orders." When you order copies of your own book, you pay just the fixed and per-page charges plus shipping and handling. CreateSpace provides a useful calculator to see your per-book cost and shipping costs.

Select "Buying Copies," and scroll down to the calculator. This will also aid you in pricing your book for sales. I recommend you read the section entitled "A few important notes about Member Orders" so you have a better understanding.

When the above mission is complete, take a break and step away to fully recharge your mind. The next mission is of massive importance and requires your full attention.

MISSION: DESCRIPTION

As I mentioned before, this is a crucial mission. To fill out your description in a strategic way means your book will rise organically using Amazon rankings. Before you compete this mission, revisit Level Six, Mission: On Target.

In our training program, we dedicate an entire module to this page. The art of cracking Amazon's code in how it ranks the information entered on this page can literally make the difference between your book becoming a bestseller and dominating its niche over the long term, or being buried under 487,000 other books where it will never been seen.

Make sure to enter information that you have studied and researched in depth. Make sure all of your language is precise and that it sings sweetly to Amazon's ranking system. Once again, I recommend you re-read Level Six, Mission: On Target before you enter any of the following information.

Description

You know what to do here. Make sure it's your best. CreateSpace shares: "The description tells potential customers about your title. The description displays in your e-Store and on your book's Amazon.com detail page, and may be used as your book's description in other sales channels you choose. Your description can have up to 4,000 characters, or about 760 words."

BISAC Category

You want to place your book into the best category to match your subject matter but which also has little competition. Chunk it down to the smallest subject area.

Where is the better place to categorize your book?

1. Self-Help > Personal Transformation
2. Advice and How-To > Health, Mind, and Body > Self-Help > Personal Transformation

Both categories are the same, yet you will have a massive advantage above the crowd if you launch your book in the second category, the winning one.

Why? Once again, it has to do with rankings. The search engines have specific behaviors and rhythms that alert Amazon, and as a result, the engine performs in a specific way. You will tend to climb up in sales in a more obvious way in the second category, whereas in the first category you will be more like a drop of rain in the ocean. This is because there is much less competition in the second way of categorizing. I call this the "nesting pattern" because it reminds me of Russian nesting dolls, where they all look the same and you keep opening them until you get to the smallest, cutest one. Most people do not know this, and their book simply gets lost on Amazon. Knowing this is a stealth bonus, which I've reserved for my coaching students in the past. Today it is my gift to you.

Enter a BISAC Code

BISAC is an acronym for Book Industry Standards and Communications. The BISAC subject heading list is an industry-approved list of subject descriptors, each of which is represented by a nine-character alphanumeric code. You can see all of the BISAC codes at the following source:

www.bisg.org/what-we-do-0-136-bisac-subject-headings-list-major-subjects.php

Before deciding on your code, make sure to go back to Amazon and check that it displays a "nesting pattern" like the second category shown above.

Author Biography

As you construct this page, it is important to make your correct brand impression. Refer back to Level Six, and construct your author bio to best position you and your brand. Make sure to include a link to your website.

Book Language

Select the language of your book.

Country of Publication

Your book's country of publication should match the information associated with your ISBN. If you are using a CreateSpace ISBN, choose the United States as your country of publication. If you are using your own ISBN, choose the country that matches the information you provided when you purchased your ISBN.

Search Keywords

Search keywords help your title show up on both Amazon.com and search engines. Pick phrases that you think customers are likely to use when searching for your title specifically or when shopping for products that may be similar in subject matter. You can add up to five keyword phrases separated by commas.

Contains Adult Content
Check here only if this book is intended for a mature audience.

Large Print
If your book is formatted for the eyesight impaired (typically with a font size of at least 16 points), your book's Amazon product detail page will be clearly marked "large print," and your book will be included in, but not limited to, the large-print book browse listings.

LEVEL EIGHT RECAP

◉ MISSION: File Upload

Uploading the Interior
Uploading the Cover
Ordering Your Proof
Mission Accomplished

◉ MISSION: Distribute

Royalty Payment Profile
Channels
Standard Distribution
Expanded Distribution
Pricing
Royalty Payments
Buying Copies for Yourself

◉ MISSION: Description

Description
BISAC Category
Enter a BISAC code
Author Biography
Book Language
Country of Publication
Search Keywords
Adult Content
Large Print

MISSION RECON

Check the mail daily; your review copy is on its way!

I must confess that it is truly AMAZING to hold your finished book in your hands! Your clients, friends, and family will also be duly impressed! They never knew that someone in their inner circle was a committed author and expert, and you will be so surprised at the response you get from people to whom you hand your book.

Once again, CONGRATULATIONS! You are the new Author Expert, ready to share your personal experiences and knowledge with the world!

LEVEL NINE

MISSION: AUTHOR IDENTITY

Your Profile

Your profile page at Amazon is where other people find you and learn more about you. This is not your author page, but it is another place where you want to align your brand.

Your profile is where you access and manage your community content. You can create new content and update your public information. You also can see your posted reviews, images, Listmania lists, and "So You'd Like To . . ." guides.

To edit your profile:

- Visit your Amazon profile page at the following: www.amazon.com/gp/pdp/profile. Log into your account if requested.
- Click the "Edit Your Profile" button on the top right-hand corner of the page.
- Update your personal information or any other settings that appear on the page.
- Click the "Save Your Profile" button when finished.

On the left side of the window, you will see a navigation pane that says "Topics." Under there you will be able to learn more about how to use your profile.

Use this tool to your advantage. Make sure all of your information is consistent with your brand identity in your other social media profiles and on your site.

Author Central

This is not the same as your profile at Amazon. Your Author Central profile is where you are highlighted as an author specifically. You will want to log in at:

authorcentral.amazon.com

On December 9, 2012, Amazon announced Author Rank, "the definitive list of best-selling authors on Amazon.com." Everything on Amazon is based on rankings, and the more you understand how their system ranks books and authors, the greater advantage you will have. Amazon strongly encourages you to add your information. From the home page you can quickly follow links to do the following:

- Update your author page.
- Add multimedia, blog feeds, a Twitter feed, or events to an Author Central profile.
- View and edit the list of your books.
- Add a book to your bibliography.
- Self-publish your work to the Kindle for free and make up to 70% in royalties.
- Join Search Inside the Book.
- Become an Amazon Associate.

There are numerous other free marketing and promotion resources at CreateSpace:

www.createspace.com/MarketingCentral/Index.jsp

At your fingertips, you'll find a variety of free marketing information and resources to help you get started and take control of your path to successfully promoting your book. We'll be adding more tools and tips, so be sure to check back for more information.

Author Page URL

Your author page URL is an easy-to-share link to your author page on Amazon.com. Use your author page URL in your email signature, blog posts, Facebook posts, and tweets. You are limited to one author page URL.

Creating your author page URL:

- On the Author Central profile tab, click add link next to "Author Page URL."
- A URL will be suggested; however, you may enter text that meets the following guidelines:

  - At least 1 character, no more than 30 characters
  - May use letters, numbers, dashes, periods, and underscores
  - No spaces
  - No special characters other than dashes, periods, and underscores
  - No profanity

- If the URL you input is available, click "Save."

Add your author page URL to your signature in your email account. Make sure that your author page aligns and stays congruent with your brand.

POSTGAME

MISSION: PROMOTION

You are going to want to match your author/book site with social media channels where you can promote your book. I recommend Facebook, Twitter, and LinkedIn. If you have a book trailer, use YouTube as well; if you don't have one, get a very creative one made for you, which will help drive sales. You will also want to plug in to your local community. By this I mean going to the local bookstores and telling them, "Hello, I'm a local author, and here is a complimentary copy of my new book. If you'd like, I can come and speak to your groups or have a book signing." Local television and radio channels, the "original social media," are always in need of fresh content—contact them! You can design your own book tour, get your book reviewed, or create a book trailer; again, you are only limited by your imagination.

The downside (if you wish to call it that) of self-publishing is that the promotion basically falls on your shoulders. In all honesty, the work you do after the book is written is more complex than actually writing the book itself. And after you have had the experience, you will never again say that writing a book is difficult or impossible; in fact pulling together the private label rights and constructing the book is the easy part!

Promoting can be easy if you're enthusiastic and willing to give it away. Give your book to reviewers, talk to people about it, etc. Just go out, have the energy, and have the feeling "I am an author; I am a star!" Think about all of the authors you like. They all began somewhere, probably in a very similar place to where you are now.

Promoting is a lot of fun if you feel proud of your work. If you feel proud of your site and all you do is start talking about it, people will come out of the woodwork to ask you about your new book.

MISSION: BOOK TRAILER

The decision to create a book trailer is entirely up to you. I can remember when "video killed the radio star" on MTV: How excited I was about some music videos (the ones that lived up to or exceeded my imagined vision of the song) and how I disliked others so much I even stopped listening to the song (the imagery just ruined it for me!). Some people argue that in a visual landscape, a book trailer is a must, while others stand firm that books should be read and not seen (unless of course it gets made into a screenplay and then a film).

The most practical advice is to trust your instincts. You know what you want to say with your book, and if it aligns congruently with your brand, then for a nonfiction book it may be a strategic move. On the other hand, it may come off as too "sales-y" and go in the opposite direction. As you can see, I still have a love/hate relationship with matching someone else's images to my own imagination. No matter what you decide, remember to keep it aligned with your brand.

You can see some interesting trailers, both engaging and horrifying, at Melville House. They host the annual Moby Awards for best and worst book trailers. Watch them here:

www.mhpbooks.com/and-the-moby-goes-to/

BookSurge has this page of trailers they have created:

www.booksurge.com/content/Video_Book_Trailer_Samples.htm

To see what book trailers look like, simply go to YouTube.com and type "book trailer" into the search box. You can search for them on Google as well.

Finally, to give you an idea about pricing, CreateSpace offers a book trailer service. Here is a link to their information:

www.createspace.com/Services/VideoBookTrailers.jsp

I created a simple trailer for my book *Reiki for Children*. In this case, I felt a visual and uplifting message to parents would be beneficial to conveying the "feeling" of my book. Here's the link:

www.ReikiKids.com

MISSION: RADIO WAVES

From Jim Green: "In October 2004, when my book *Your Retirement Masterplan* (How To Books, ISBN 1857039874) was published, I participated in eleven 15-minute live interviews on local radio over a period of just five days. The results were highly encouraging; the book leapt from nowhere on Amazon.co.uk to position 194 out of 3123 competing titles and eventually grabbed the #1 spot for its core keyword (retirement) where it remained for nine months."

So what if you self-publish but you don't have a publicist to arrange radio interviews? Does that mean you're excluded? No way! Wherever you live in the world, you'll find that the majority of local radio stations are banded together into a single network for cost-effectiveness.

Here is what you do:

1. Identify the controlling network.
2. Visit the corporate website containing links to all subsidiaries.
3. Pick out those stations within a 500–1000 mile radius.
4. Visit each local station website individually.
5. Scan the daily programming schedules.
6. Highlight those programs that might identify with the topic of your book.
7. Note the presenter's name.
8. Email the presenter with a well-couched request for a live interview.
9. Follow that up with an identical snail-mail request.
10. Follow that up with a telephone call (you'll get to speak to someone in authority).

You know your topic inside and out. Speak up with confidence, and you'll get your interview; maybe not straightaway, but if you sell yourself and your project professionally, you'll be logged into an up-and-coming slot in the station scheduling. The only investment in this is your time—or you could outsource the work.

MISSION: GIVE AWAY

Christine Kling, a former professor at Broward College, discovered and utilized the Amazon Select program. This program allows authors to give away some of their books for free as promotions in exchange for agreeing to go exclusively with the online retailer. She targeted sites that advertise free books, figuring, "If they list free books they might buy another." When she tried this strategy the first time, readers downloaded more than 37,000 free copies of her book *Circle of Bones* in only three days. But what happened next is an example of paying things forward at its best, because word of mouth in the age of social media is a beautiful thing. In the following 30 days, Christine sold 8,000 books.

Amazon pays its authors a 70% royalty rate. She was selling her book for $3.99. Doing the math, she made more that month than she made working as a college professor.

There are e-readers like Kindle, Nook, Sony Reader, and devices like the iPad. People can now read your work on their mobile phones as well as online. Amazon stated on their website, "For the third week in a row, customers are purchasing well over 1 million Kindle devices per week." Book sales have been soaring, and sales for self-published authors have been on the rise, with many surpassing the rates of traditionally published authors.

MISSION: BONUS BOOK LAUNCH

There are various ways to promote your book, but if you're really aiming for going to the top of Amazon, then there's one method for sure-fire success: having a bonus book launch.

There are professionals who elegantly and seamlessly coordinate all of the parts and players so you can focus on what you do (being an author/expert). I recommend that if you want to launch a book, you do so professionally. It is a lot of work, and ideally you will need to plan this at least three to four months out.

I'm sure you have seen bonus book launch pages. You arrive at a website (usually matched to the name of the book), and the first thing you see is the book cover or book trailer. You will see some endorsements or reviews and information about the author. There is either a "Buy The Book Now" or a "Reserve Your Copy" button. Somewhere prominently shown on the page will be a bonus announcement.

Some go over the top with claims like "Buy the book today and get over $5,000 in bonuses!" I recommend that you use the "less is more" philosophy. While this exaggerated tactic may have worked in the past, it has been quite overused and can appear tasteless. If you do it elegantly, it can work to your advantage in a powerful way.

The primary idea is that if you buy the book you will also be able to claim additional bonuses. I recommend working with a few but well-known bonus partners. Make sure the gifts they contribute are unique and provide value to your customers. I do not have to remind you that everything you put out needs to be congruent and aligned with your brand.

Stacking Value

What is the purpose of doing a bonus book launch?

It is a strategy called "stacking value." What happens is that you stack so much value on the original product that potential customers cannot resist the bargain of getting so much for so little. In other words, the purchaser is thinking, "Wow, I'm going to buy this book for only $14.95, and I'm going to get all of these other things!" The decision to buy, when presented that way, becomes a no-brainer. The deal sounds so good that they buy on impulse. They get your book and a whole lot of other information to boot.

Building the List

Another benefit to you is that you can create a page where the purchaser goes to collect the bonuses. If you plan strategically and make this an opt-in page, you are now gaining all of those email addresses and building your list.

The benefit to the partners who are offering a bonus is that they also create an opt-in box for the purchaser to download their bonus gift, so they also build their list in the process.

I am sure you've heard that "the money is in the list." When you have captured your purchasers' email address, you can continue to market and sell to that customer.

The primary strategy is that your list, combined with the email lists of all partners, sends a well-coordinated and orchestrated series of mailings prompting people to go to Amazon on the same day of your launch to buy your book. This immediately raises your rankings, and the book begins to move towards #1.

JOINT VENTURES

You work together for a common goal: getting the book to #1 and collecting email addresses, which builds you and your partners' lists. I have just defined the term "joint venture," or JV.

So how does it work?

It is a win–win–win strategy if done right.

The Author
You win by having a mass of traffic, attention, and "buzz" in the days leading to the launch and on launch day. Aside from obvious book sales, Amazon is very busy on launch day with promoting your title, and that often makes you climb towards bestseller status. Your credibility is boosted with the alignment of your expert partners. Opt-in for gifts grows your marketing list. You build powerful relationships with other experts and authors.

Aligned Expert Partner
By offering a bonus or gift you are exposed to people who otherwise may not be in your audience. Your credibility is boosted with the alignment of your expert partners. Opt-in options for gifts grow your marketing list. You build powerful relationships with other experts and authors.

Book Purchaser
They win because not only do they get an awesome book, they also gain exclusive access to many bonuses and gifts. This is the ultimate reward for purchasing on a specific day.

The Power of We

Because everyone is aligned to send emails, tweets, Facebook posts, etc. on the same day to collect the gifts, there is a great buzz around the popularity of the book. Intelligently designed book launches use images, have pre-written tweets, strategically placed Facebook status updates, and more. But the real power of a JV bonus book launch comes when everyone emails their list, making a personal recommendation for the book. Depending on how many partners participate, there can be as many as a million emails circulating in cyberspace on the day of your launch. Now imagine the super power of everyone tweeting and posting about your book too! This is teamwork at its best!

It is the combined power of everyone with the same goal (to get the book to #1) that triggers Amazon's rankings to go to work, and your book moves at lightning speed.

Finally, consider creating a special bonus product you can offer to participating authors on their launches. Reciprocity is a wonderful thing and will strengthen the bonds with your author and expert peers.

I recommend you strongly consider the option of hiring a book launch professional and remember the super power of working together, especially in this day and age of social community. Once again, the three I can personally recommend are located in the Resources section at the back of the book. Tell them I sent you and to take good care of you!

AFFIRMATIVE ACTIONS

Go over all of your notes and formulate a plan of action for the next 30 days:

- Get the website done.
- Consider a book trailer and have it done.
- Locate local bookstores and initiate personal relationship.
- Strategize what product(s) can evolve out of the book.

So, here we are at the end of this book, but also the beginning of *your* book! I have given you all of the information, links, resources, tips, shortcuts, contacts, and advice. From this point forward, the rest is up to you. My closing piece of advice is "Just get Started." If you get stuck, we do have a coaching program that can help you overcome any obstacle. Just visit our site:

www.BeMoreThanYouAre.com/coaching

AFTERWORD

One of the things I most try to get across to my authors is the need to build a platform, and to build their brand through their platform as they write their book or as they promote their book). And I urge them to do this in a step-by-step, logical manner.

Most people look at me with alarm when I explain to them they need to do something beyond writing their book. They thought the work was finished when they ran their manuscript through spell-check. Most people, and authors are among them, don't want to take the time to invest in themselves! They want others to do it for them. But it'll pay off in the end if you trust in yourself enough to give yourself time to grow.

As you have seen, Kytka Hilmar-Jezek makes doing it for yourself more enjoyable than not. Becoming a brand in yourself, becoming an authority in your field, becoming the author who gets noticed all take hard work. But that doesn't mean the hard work is drudgery. On the contrary, it's really fulfilling. I've published my own book, and I've done a lot of heavy lifting—but I didn't do it alone.

Kytka shows you how to gather together a team and how to have fun building your brand. She has taken a lot of the things I teach my authors, and that I've taught and explained to students, and created her own book.

Here you've got a plan of action.

Use it.

—Michael R. Drew

Since the age of nineteen, **Michael R. Drew** has become a leading book marketer in the publishing industry, propelling nearly 75 books onto national bestseller lists, including The Wall Street Journal, USA Today and The New York Times, and garnering over 1,000 #1 rankings for books on Amazon. com through his Promote A Book services. Michael heads a marketing agency that strives to build strong and real relationships with his clients and their audiences, increasing sales in a natural manner, and maximizing the depth and longevity of that relationship through its Persona Architecture and Platform Building programs. Michael has presented the Pendulum theory on stage with and for the Dali Lama, Sir Richard Branson, and Steven R. Covey, and privately for the Executive Committee at Franklin Covey.

ATTACHÉ CASE

ABOUT THE AUTHOR

Meet author and business mentor Kytka Hilmar-Jezek. Kytka is the CEO of Be More Network. A born entrepreneur and #1 bestselling author of numerous books, including her latest, *BOOK POWER: A Platform for Writing, Branding, Positioning & Publishing*, Kytka has built over 125 websites and 10 successful businesses online and off.

She has successfully catapulted countless entrepreneurs to superstar success. From her online coaching programs to live masterminds and private mentoring, Kytka offers training for big-thinking entrepreneurs who want proven strategies and guidance to monetize their greatest ideas while living their fullest lives.

A strong advocate of alternative education and young entrepreneurs, Kytka is the proud parent of three children who are enjoying a life of freedom by creatively capitalizing on their passions to create businesses and products that offer them a lifetime of royalties and passive income.

RESOURCES

Aligned Book Promotions
You can see by the titles/authors which genre best represents each Book Launch expert.

Denise Cassino
www.BestSellerServices.com

Track Record:
Rosanna Lenco, *Awakening the Divine Soul*
Cindy Ashton, *Kiss Your Monster Goodbye*
Dr. Anna Maria Prezio, *Confessions of a Feng Shui Ghost Buster*
Ping Li, *Awakening, Fulfilling Your Soul's Purpose on Earth*
Bernadette Boas, *Shedding the Corporate Bitch*
Don Staley, *Fit Mind, Fit Body*
Dr. Walter E. Jacobson, *Forgive to Win*
Tanya Denckla Cobb, *Reclaiming Our Food*

Judy O'Beirn
www.HasmarkServices.com

Track Record:
Deepak Chopra, Debbie Ford, Marianne Williamson,
    The Shadow Effect
Marci Shimoff, *Happy for No Reason*
Judith Orloff, MD, *Emotional Freedom*
Peggy McColl, *Your Destiny Switch*
Gregg Braden, *The Spontaneous Healing of Belief*
Jerry and Esther Hicks, *Money and the Law of Attraction*
Arielle Ford, *Wabi Sabi Love*

Barbara Marx Hubbard, *Birth 2012 and Beyond*

Jack Canfield and William Gladstone, *The Golden Motorcycle Gang*

Arielle Ford, *The Soulmate Secret*

Robin Sharma, *The Leader Who Had No Title*

Judith Orloff MD, *Second Sight*

Immaculee Ilibagiza, *Led by Faith*

Ariane de Bonvoisin, *The First 30 Days*

Bill Bartmann, *Bailout Riches! How Everyday Investors Can Make a Fortune Buying Bad Loans for Pennies on the Dollar*

Michael Drew
www.PromoteABook.com

Track Record:

Michael excels with 74 out of 74 launches that were each bestsellers on an average of four major national bestseller lists.

John Assaraf, *The Street Kid's Guide to Having It All*

Bryan Eisenberg and Jeffrey Eisenberg, *Call To Action: Secret Formulas to Improve Online Results*

T. Harv Eker, *Secrets of the Millionaire Mind: Mastering the Inner Game of Wealth*

Loral Lengemeier, *The Millionaire Maker's Guide to Wealth Cycle Investing*

Lisa Nichols, *No Matter What*

Keller Williams, *Shift*

RECOMMENDED READING

- *Start With Why* **by Simon Sinek**
  Drawing on a wide range of real-life stories, Sinek weaves together a clear vision of what it truly takes to lead and inspire.

- *The Millionaire Messenger: Make a Difference and a Fortune Sharing Your Advice* **by Brendon Burchard**
  In the industry of people who share their advice and knowledge with the world and get paid for it, Burchard is the "guru's guru." If you've ever wondered how the gurus spread their message, serve others, and build a real business, then this is a must-read.

- *Crush It* **by Gary Vaynerchuk**
  One day Gary turned on a video camera, and by using the secrets revealed in this book, transformed his entire life and earning potential by building his personal brand. "Everything has changed." The social media revolution has irreversibly changed the way we live our lives and conduct our business. Billions of dollars in advertising are moving online, waiting to be claimed by whoever can build the best content and communities.

- *Pendulum: How Past Generations Shape Our Present and Predict Our Future* **by Roy H. Williams and Michael R. Drew**
  An incredible study on markets, trends, and the 40-year cycles behind the shifts. The authors discuss how we move back and forth between "me" and "we" cycles and how this movement affects everything in culture. A must for anyone interested in marketing and branding in a way to communicate intimately with your clients' innermost feelings and creating products and services that really meet their needs. An awesome and interesting read.

- *Book Yourself Solid: The Fastest, Easiest, and Most Reliable System for Getting More Clients Than You Can Handle Even if You Hate Marketing and Selling* by Michael Port
  If you're even slightly uncomfortable with the idea of networking, marketing, or selling, this is the book for you.

- *The 22 Immutable Laws of Branding* by Al and Laura Ries
  This is the definitive text on branding. It provides you with pairing anecdotes about some of the best brands in the world, like Rolex, Volvo, Starbucks, and Heineken.

- *Emotional Branding: The New Paradigm for Connecting Brands to People* by Marc Gobe
  A great book that shows marketers of any product or service how to engage with today's increasingly cynical consumers on deeper emotional levels.

- *Unleashing the IdeaVirus* by Seth Godin
  Recognizes the importance of new ideas, change, and innovation within product or services.

- *Experiential Marketing* by Bernd H. Schmitt
  From Amtrak and Singapore Airlines to Herbal Essences products and Gwyneth Paltrow, you will find a revolutionary approach to marketing for the branding and information age.

- *Building Strong Brands* by David A. Aaker
  This book will show you how to deal with the fragmentation of markets by building brand identity, creating brand personality, and managing a brand system. Real case scenarios including General Electric, Healthy Choice, McDonald's, and others to demonstrate how strong brands are created and managed.

- *Likeable Social Media* by **Dave Kerpen**
  Reveals the remarkable returns you'll get when you gain the trust of your customers, which is what branding is all about.

- *Designing Brand Identity* by **Alina Wheeler**
  Provides a practical structure for the brand-building process. A powerful and inspiring toolkit to get started.

- *We, Me, Them & It* by **John Simmons**
  A compelling case for a unique brand voice.

- *Managing Brand Equity* by **David Aaker**
  Timeless principles. An oldie but a goodie.

- *The Pirate Inside* by **Adam Morgan**
  It's about a lot more than a logo: It's about what you represent and why.

- *Me 2.0: Build a Powerful Brand to Achieve Career Success* by **Dan Schawbel**
  Dan is the leading personal branding expert for Gen-Y. An effective four-step process for discovering, creating, communicating, and maintaining a personal brand.

- *Career Distinction: Stand Out by Building Your Brand* by **William Arruda and Kirsten Dixson**
  Career Distinction demonstrates how to express who you are, the value you bring to your organization, and how to brand you as an indispensable, memorable, and unique professional. Success takes more than just hard work; brand yourself and watch your career soar.

- *U R a Brand! How Smart People Brand Themselves for Business Success* by **Catherine Kaputa**
  Strategies and tactics to tap into the power of words, learn the principles of visual identity, think in terms of markets, and execute a self-brand action plan that is unique and memorable.

- *Be Your Own Brand: A Breakthrough Formula for Standing Out from the Crowd* by **David McNally and Karl D. Speak**
  Developing a personal brand is not about constructing a contrived image. Rather, it is a process of discovering who you really are and what you aspire to be. The hallmark insight of the new edition is that the best way to establish a strong and memorable brand is to make a positive difference in the lives of others through making lasting impressions that build trusting relationships.

- *The Brand Called You: Create a Personal Brand That Wins Attention and Grows Your Business* by **Peter Montoya and Tim Vandehey**
  Oprah. Martha Stewart. Charles Schwab. They've built their success around their personal brands. This book will help you to build and maintain a personal brand. It also teaches you how to craft an emotionally resonant branding message, create top-quality branding tools, and attract a consistent flow of business.

Do More. Live More. Be More.

Made in the USA
Lexington, KY
11 November 2013